Pathway to Personal Freedom and Love

A personal guide for a healthier,
happier you through love,
positive thinking, and behavior.

by

D.R. HUNT aka DR Love

First published in January 1992 under the title *Learn to Love* by First Pocket Book.

2nd Edition, 2017, title *Pathway to Personal Freedom and Love*, manufactured in USA

2 3 4 5 6 7 8 9 10 LSI 22 21 20 19 18 17
Set in Palatino, Times New Roman, and Zapfino

Photograph on the front cover is in the public domain.

International Standard Book Number: 978-0-692-87189-8

Drlovedavid.com
Pathwaytofreedomandlove.com
dr.dave6948@gmail.com

Dedicated to the memory of
Dr. Isolde "Miriamme" Czukor,
who unselfishly shared
her love, her light, her life with all mankind.

NAMASTE

CONTENTS

FOREWORD

This is a diet book full of recipes and poems for aligning MIND, BODY and SOUL with its true self for the expressed mission of discovering and fulfilling your purpose and destiny.

It explains how to unlock the inner door of one's self to unchain the fears that bind and to set free the light of forgiveness to nullify the darkness of judgment through the joys of Love for everlasting peace, joy and tranquility.

This book is likened to a rare well-chosen and well-tended fruit tree. Its fruits are not for one season only. With due and natural intervals, it can be recurred to year after year, and it will supply the same nourishment and the same gratification, if only one returns to it with the same healthy appetite.

YOU are writing a book,
a new chapter each day,
by deeds that you do,
by words that you say.
Whether faithless or true,
men read what you write,
so write what you mean,
according to you.

AUTHOR'S NOTE

Being healthy and happy is a natural state, and the means for achieving it are within the grasp of each of us. A judicious mixture of clear thinking, humor, self-confidence, and love are the ingredients for productive and joyous living. Love is the catalyst that binds the threads of life within us and us with the universe.

For those readers with a religious background, you may prefer substituting the word GOD for the word Love or the word Universe, for these words have been interchanged throughout this book. For GOD is Love and the creator of the Universe, and all is one.

I hope the following pages will be as inspiring and as enjoyable for you as they were for me in creating them.

Let the light of Love
Shine brightly forever
Guiding your way

INTRODUCTION

Pathway to Personal Freedom and Love is a book to be used, not just read. This book defines love and relationships. It offers guidelines for value placing, granting freedom, and respecting integrity. It will assist in letting go of fears, such as guilt, worry, and procrastination. It will help build esteem, worth, and confidence. It will demonstrate how positive thinking will produce positive results, thus paving the way for a more peaceful and tranquil way of living.

This book is not presented as a substitute for therapy. If you feel the need, do not hesitate to seek professional help. The fact that you are reading these pages demonstrates that you are interested in being a healthy, positive person.

Congratulations!

Pathway to Personal Freedom and Love

Chapter 1
Today a Fresh Start

A NEW BEGINNING

Today can be a fresh start for the rest of your life by thinking positive thoughts within your mind, by loving from your heart, and by eliminating negative behavior from your lifestyle.

Positive behavior is living in the present and being free from the chains of fear that inhibit you from living with peace, joy, and prosperity.

Positive thinking is believing that all things are possible and that what you think and what you believe will manifest itself within and around you.

Positive thinking is necessary, but it is just as important that your thinking be focused. You create this focus by defining your purpose, and by concentrating enough faith on your purpose so that it will manifest itself in your world.

Purpose is your conscious mind discovering truths about your beingness, which your Higher-Self has known all along.

Eventually you will recognize that your purpose is seeing and feeling the perfection of what is, just the way it is. You will further recognize that your knowingness will create your life just the way it is so that you may embrace it in love and make it a part of you.

When you align all of your thoughts with your purpose, life will look different. You will notice that everything will have meaning and will support you. And that the light of Love will spring forth illuminating the shadows making all things clear.

Love is accepting others without criticism, and finding peace and harmony within yourself and within the universe.

Peaceful and joyous living is a matter of choice. **THINKING, BELIEVING,** and **DOING** [with love, having a purpose, and focusing on that purpose] are the keys to a healthy and joyful life.

Today is the first day of the rest of your life. You have been given this day to use as you will. You can waste it or you can use it for good. When tomorrow comes this day will be gone forever, leaving yesterday in its place. You have exchanged a day of your life for it. What you do today is very important. Do you want it to be gain or loss, good or evil, success or failure?

Begin **TODAY** creating positive thoughts, building confidence, loving yourself, and loving all that is within the universe.

You will be faced with a series of great adventures brilliantly disguised as impossible situations just waiting to be conquered with enthusiasm and love. Each day is an opportunity for you to start anew by cleansing your heart and mind, by clarifying your vision and by making sure that today is not cluttered up with worthless baggage of yesterday.

Enjoy life, for each day brings a constant demonstration of power and beauty from the universe and from within yourself. And, what you think of yourself is the most important opinion of all.

Go forth with each new day,
having faith and confidence in you,
and you'll find that your fears
will disappear from view.

Go forth with faith in your heart
and mind, with confidence anew,
and there's nothing in this world
you'll find, that you cannot do.

Look at the bright side of life,
cast out gloom and despair,
look within your heart and mind, and
you'll find love and knowledge there.

Chapter 2

Positive Thinking

HAVE A GOAL

POSITIVE THOUGHTS CREATE POSITIVE RESULTS

Be confident, no matter what obstacle or undesirable circumstance crosses your path. Refuse to accept the negative, for it is nothing but an illusion. Error and evil are the results of your thoughts, and negative thoughts must not be allowed to clutter your mind. Hold your thoughts steadfastly on the good. Do not dwell on negative thoughts or on past events. Do this with ease, do not command it, simply relax in the contemplation of the good.

Refuse to accept evil, and evil is gone. Accept only the good, and a constant supply of love from the universe is yours. Know that all things are the result of conception and desire, that your world is ordered according to your thoughts and convictions.

THOUGHT PLUS BELIEF CREATES

Your thoughts cross your mind in a never-ending stream. You may choose any thought that you so desire. As you accept your thoughts, so will they manifest in your world. You alone will decide what you will think and what you will believe, thus deciding your destiny.

Happiness, health, abundance, and success are all yours, if you choose only such thoughts. You need neither to accept nor to reject your thoughts. If you so desire, you may place your thoughts on hold to be reviewed at a later date when understanding proves itself through time.

Let go of fear and confusion, for they are illusions that cannot live with truth. Surrender all inhibitions that have been impressed upon you by the illusions of the world. Refuse to accept anything but truth, which is the good and the positive.

Let reality govern your every thought and let truth be the master of your fate. Focus your thoughts on the truth and allow truth to become the creator of your reality.

TREAT OTHERS AS YOU WOULD LIKE TO BE TREATED

Do not use this idiom! This rule allows the givers to be taken advantage of by the takers. It also increases the possibility for the givers to create hurt feelings within themselves when their good deeds and kind thoughts are not appreciated or returned. Another shortcoming of this rule is that others might assume that you do not have any needs or wants, because all they see is you giving to others and not doing for yourself.

TREAT YOURSELF AS YOU WOULD LIKE OTHERS TO TREAT YOU

Use this rule! This rule allows you to take care of yourself first, which then gives you a better foundation in taking care of others if need be. It also allows for you to be less vulnerable to hurt feelings when others do not appreciate your kind deeds or thoughts. It will also be more apparent to others that you have needs and desires, and it will be easier for others to identify those needs. Another advantage of this rule is that your needs and desires will be satisfied more often by treating yourself first.

Lack and limitation are only errors of thinking. Know that abundance and creativity are mental conditions. You need only to open your mind and to believe from your heart, and you will be filled with abundance and love from the universe.

Life is a journey to be travelled step-by-step with patience, enjoying the wonders along the way with unshakable faith towards your destination.

I am that I am
wherever I go
wherever I am
I am
at the center
of the universe;
as I move
so does the center
therefore
the universe
revolves
around me.

I am
a part
of the universe
and
I am
the universe;
for
all is one.

My mind
has no limits;
therefore
I must fulfill
my own destiny
by expanding
my consciousness
to the point
where
I am one
with
all creation.

Open your heart to love, and love will flow throughout your very being; energizing, molding, and coordinating. Say it to yourself, *"I am now qualifying every electron that leaves my heart and flows into my blood stream with the immaculate concept of regeneration and rejuvenation of eternal youth and absolute perfection for every cell in my body."*

By cleansing your mind of negative thoughts, you will automatically cleanse your body. Your body is simply an instrument of expression, and your ego is simply the memory of your physical experience.

Be patient, for you have the power to allocate and to control your time and space. Be wise, for you have the ability to seek knowledge. Be rich, for there is no limit to abundance. You create from your very self. Be successful, for you need only to think to achieve.

Love others and allow yourself to be loved, for all things are yourself, and you are all things. You need never to wear the mask of vanity again. Perceive the magnificent dweller at the center of your soul, and you will know him to be yourself. Time and space, shadow and substance, what matter these?

YOU ARE WHO YOU BELIEVE YOU ARE

When you have gained a constant awareness of love, you will have gained all that there is in this world. All that this world is, you are, and all that you are is all that there is. Your mind can move easily to the farthermost reaches of space in all directions and just as easily move back again: For you are the center of the universe, and as the center you are empowered to magnify love, for you are an instrument of Love.

Where there is hatred, sow love
Where there is despair, present hope
Where there is sadness, contribute joy

Seek not to be loved but to love
Seek not to be forgiven but to forgive
Seek not to be consoled but to console
Seek not to be understood but to understand

It is in giving that you receive
It is in loving that you are loved
It is in respecting that you are respected
It is in pardoning that you are pardoned
It is in granting freedom that you are free

Biblical Beatitudes

Chapter 3
Perception of Love

FIND IT WITHIN

Love is the passionate and abiding desire on the part of two or more people to produce together conditions under which each can be, and spontaneously express, one's real self; to produce together an intellectual soil and an emotional climate in which each can flourish, far superior to what either could achieve alone.

Love is accepting others without criticism, recognizing their perfection, and not changing them to fit a particular mold.

The basic qualities of love are **COMPASSION, TRUST,** and **ESTEEM.**

COMPASSION MEANS TO SUFFER WITH. It links understanding, sorrow, and forgiveness with a desire to comfort others with tenderness and kindness.

TRUST RELATES TO EXPOSING ONE'S INNER SELF. It commits one to confidence, integrity, justice, and friendship without limits or consequences, allowing for mistakes and freedom.

ESTEEM IS TO VALUE HIGHLY. It connects faith with respect, appreciation, honesty, admiration, and reverence, which will aid you when making appraisals or setting values.

Have patience, faith, and trust. Know that all human problems can be resolved through love. Love is given freely, without restrictions, and with understanding, not doubt. Love is honesty, not deceit, and creativity, not conditioning. Fear (doubt) is the absence of faith, a destroyer of love. Trust and forgiveness are steps in granting freedom and reestablishing lost love.

Love is friendship evolving from mutual respect. It is quiet understanding, sharing, and forgiving. It is loyalty through good and bad times. It is acknowledging perfection, and recognizing that the appearance of weakness is only an error in perception.

Love is being content with the present, having faith in the future, and not brooding over the past. It is sharing and working together on the day-in and day-out problems, irritations, compromises, disappointments, victories, and common goals.

If you have love in your heart, it will make up for a quality that you may lack. But if you do not have love in your heart, no matter what else is there, it will not be enough.

Know that your purpose in life is to expand in knowledge and to cultivate love, becoming one with the universe. Open your mind, believe from your heart, and love will flow throughout your very being.

There are two main perspectives. **LOVE**, your natural inheritance. And **FEAR**, an illusory invention of your mind. You cannot change your mind by changing your behavior. But you can change your behavior by changing your thinking and focusing on positive results.

You choose the thoughts that you experience, and everything that happens to you, you create. It is up to you to take control of your mind, and then practice feeling and behaving the way in which you aspire.

He drew a circle that shut me out,
But Love and I had the wit to win,
We drew a bigger circle that took him in.

It is in loving, not in being loved,
that the heart is blessed.
It is in giving, not in seeking gifts,
that we find our quest.

Whatever be the longing
or need that give;
So shall the soul be fed,
and you indeed shall live.

Above all worldly advice
If I could tell just one thing,
one meaningful thing
I thought was worth remembering,

I would truly say love
with all your soul and heart,
continuing forever and
ever, until least you depart.

Chapter 4
Value Placing

IT'S YOU, NOT THEM

Isolate motives from words because words have no power except that which you give to them. It is not people that hurt you, but the value that you place upon the action and reactions of others. If you understand that what disturbs you is only the result of your value placing, you will flow with situations and stay emotionally uninvolved.

Do not criticize, condemn, or judge others, nor should you bestow your state of mind upon others as well. It is not what happens to you, good or bad, but how you react to the happening and what you gain from the experience that matters.

It is reprehensible to place the responsibility for your happiness upon others. True happiness is found only in the bosom of one's self.

If there is one lesson or thought that you cannot readily understand, then put that thought aside. Do not accept or reject that thought until understanding grows and expands, and has proven itself through time.

It is not what anyone says or does that affects you, it is the value that you give to the actions of others that acts upon you.

If you believe that someone is interfering or upsetting you in any way, just step aside and reflect. Remember that nothing others say or do will bother you unless you allow it. The reactions that you create will be determined by the values that you place.

If someone makes a comment that you would consider reacting negatively, just say, *"that's your opinion and that's OK, our views are just different."* Do not get upset or attempt to change their opinions because it will be a futile effort. Opinions change when one's state of mind changes. Actually, your values can change in a few days, weeks, or even overnight.

Sun light, Sun bright
I'll love today with all my might.
Star light, Star bright
I'll find peace within me tonight.

The energy that you send out, as in value placing, is like a boomerang with a magnet. What you send out will return to you, picking up similar energy from others, then returning that loaded energy to you. If someone gives you a present (vile names, accusations, etc.) and you do not accept or place a value upon it, then that negative energy will bypass you and will return straight to the sender.

Refrain from blaming, cursing, and judging others, because that negative energy will return, often causing pain and suffering. You are entitled to your own opinions, but it is not necessary to accept the burden of negative opinions from others.

Be at peace with yourself. By loving yourself, you will be able to return the energy of love, even when others send out hate and anger. Learn to change the value or the polarization of negative energy directed towards you.

Do not register anything less than good from the experiences of the day so that your rest and sleep will remain undisturbed. Finding peace, harmony, and the feeling of unity with the universe will instill tranquility within you.

From this point forth, grant yourself the authority to regulate your life in accordance with your overall purpose: Everything in your life shall, from this moment, fall into its proper place. Each and every condition, desire, and circumstance is in its proper place, even the concept of yourself. If any part of you is not in alignment with the true you, then change in whatever way or manner that is best to align you with your true self. This should be your highest commitment.

Look to the rainbow
filled with love today,
and toward the stars
to brighten your way.

Look for the beauty
and goodness in all,
finding yourself erect
and standing tall.

Discover love throughout
the mighty universe,
finding peace and harmony
rich in golden verse.

Inspired by:
Roger Whittaker Song

Chapter 5
Granting Freedom

GRANTING FREEDOM IS FORGIVING AND FORGIVING IS LETTING GO

Grant freedom to everyone around you. Then claim freedom for yourself. Do not claim freedom of thought, feeling, or action for yourself until you have given freedom to all those around you.

You must not impose upon others your ideas or your beliefs until help is asked for. If you err in making choices for another, especially if it turns out poorly, you must then accept the burden and the responsibility of your action.

If you cannot reach the point of giving freedom, then inevitably you will lose that which you are trying to hold. Give complete freedom to others, and love will begin to flow freely and unconditionally.

To grant freedom to someone you might say, *"You are free to come and go as you please. All I am giving to you is what I am claiming for myself."* You must give freedom to others before granting freedom for yourself.

That which belongs to you will not leave you. Arbitrarily holding onto someone or something, because of your fear of losing that person or thing, will cut you off from that which belongs to you or that which would have otherwise come to you freely. Giving freedom completely, without qualification, will draw all that is helpful from people, events, and conditions.

Place another into bondage and you will go into bondage. As you go into bondage, you will experience increasing misery, agony, and suffering, mainly from egotistical pride. Practice giving freedom. Nothing that belongs to you will leave you. All that belongs to you will flow unto you. You will not lose anything that is yours.

There is joy and happiness in giving freedom. Each night upon retiring, review the events of the day to see whether in action or in thought that you have given freedom to everyone with whom you are associated. When you experience the joy and happiness that comes with giving freedom, then claim it for yourself.

However, when you actually begin to claim freedom for yourself, you may be accused by others of being heartless because you will no longer allow others to control you.

Those who wish to hold you in bondage for their own selfish reasons may appeal to your sympathy. If they can no longer dominate you or reach you through fear, they will attempt to crawl into your heart through sympathy. Sympathy is a very insidious weapon that can enslave us all, and is habitually used when all other weapons fail.

Be most alert and perceptive, for the individuals who apply sympathy will put on a terrific act. To counteract this situation, confront that individual with their dilemma and explain to them that you desire to understand more.

You must acknowledge the opinions of others rather than confronting them with your beliefs, acknowledging that understanding starts from one's state of development. This does not mean that you endorse their beliefs. You merely give freedom for others to grow according to their state of development, requirements, and needs. Now you are free to tread your path according to your own needs and goals.

If you love it, set it free
If it returns it was meant to be
If it stays away let it be
If you love it, you set it free

Sometimes you must be stern in letting go of those holding you in bondage. Tell them, *"My happiness comes from within me, not from you, not only because you may be temporary, but because you want me to be what I am not."* Or, say, *"I cannot be happy when I change merely to satisfy your selfishness, nor do I feel content when you criticize me for not thinking your thoughts or for not seeing things the same as you. You call me a rebel, yet each time that I have expressed my beliefs, you have rebelled against me. I do not attempt to mold your mind, I know that you are striving just to be you, and I cannot allow you to tell me what to be, for I am concentrating very hard on being just me. It is difficult for me to be around you at this time, because I am trying very hard to improve my self-image, and to control the way in which I allow others to treat me."*

I can see clearly now, the snow has gone.
I see my obstacles all melting away.
Gone are the dark clouds that had me blind.
It's going to be a bright, sunshiny day.

I can see clearly now, the rain has cleared.
I see my troubles all draining away.
Look straight ahead, there's nothing but blue skies.
It's going to be a bright, bright rainbow day.

I can make it now, the pain has gone.
All of my bad feelings have drifted away.
Now is the rainbow that I have been looking for.
It's going to be a bright, bright loving day.

The future is bright, the darkness has gone.
My spirits are high, bad memories have faded away.
Look all around, there's nothing but blue skies.
It's going to be a bright, bright sunny day.

Inspired by:
Roger Whittaker song

LETTING GO

Sifting through the ashes of our relationship, I find many things to be grateful for. I can say, *"Thank you"* for warm mornings, terrific meals, and all the love that you have ever offered. I can say, *"Thank you"* for being there, willing to be shared, for the many poems that you were the inspiration for, and for the many changes that I have made within my life.

I can say, *"Thank you"* for fond memories, and for the joy of forgiveness and forbearance. You were the best and worst of loves, and you left behind several unintended gifts. Through you, I have re-examined my needs and my desires for the one significant other to share my life with.

You commanded in me an unwilling re-evaluation of self, behavior, relationships, and a corresponding change in attitudes. I am more in touch with feelings, things, and people around me. And, of course, a scattering of poems, the best and the worst, which would never have been without your disruption.

The need for you still remains, but less and less you seem the way to fulfill that need. May you be blessed with health, happiness, and prosperity, now and forevermore * **NAMASTE** * God bless the divinity in you.

Chapter 6
Respecting Integrity

HONOR YOUR NEIGHBOR

Respect is feeling or showing honor towards another and revealing your appreciation. It is holding someone in high regard and showing consideration to them.

Respect the integrity of everyone. Respect precedes all healthy love. If you lose the respect of man, woman, or child, you may lose their love. No one can substitute lost respect. When loving or being loved, demonstrate your respect by being considerate and compassionate.

You must also have respect for yourself, or you will resent your very being. Preserve the respect of those you wish to love, and you will encourage their love.

Respect the integrity of all those around you in your daily life, respecting their privacy and their possessions, as well as respecting their quirks and their idiosyncrasies. Because you, too, have faults and shortcomings that they contend with. You are merely displaying your egotism when you demand others to be like yourself or as you would prefer them to be. Allowing them to live their life according to their own needs and goals is paramount.

If you do not lose patience or overwhelm others with your desire to help and you do not act overly emotional over their situation, others will confide in you what their needs are.

Do not attempt to superimpose your ideas or your beliefs upon others unless help is asked for. Be attentive, respecting the integrity of others. Learn their needs, and learn to function with them.

If you are too aggressive in your desire to help, you will prevent others from confiding in or accepting your help. Do not become discouraged if others do not accept your help immediately. They may not be ready to confide in anyone just yet. They may need more time to build a trusting relationship.

Remember that others have their own needs and requirements that are not the same as yours. Respecting yourself and all those around you will foster love for yourself as well as for all those around you.

Respect is honoring thy neighbor
with fruits of thy mind and labor.
Sow courtesy, consideration and passion
reaping the peace and joy of compassion.
Transplant the faults of others
using the forgiveness of mothers.
Sprinkle with some light from above
bringing forth new blossoms of love.
Nurture and protect thy neighbor
when help is by them requested for.
Be observant, for thy thoughtful deeds
may not satisfy another's perceived needs.
Respect thy own leaves, branches and trunk,
nurturing thy self for maintaining thy spunk.
Cultivate thy roots, stems and crown
for thou art the most worthy, in town.

". . . creation of woman from the rib of man: She was not made of his head to top him; nor out of his feet to be trampled by him; but out of his side to be equal with him; and under his arm to be protected by him; and near his heart to be Loved by him."

Chapter 7
Man/Woman/Gorilla

WHAT'S THE DIFFERENCE?

If you study the characteristics of Men, Women, and Primates [mainly the largest of the ape family, the gorilla] you would find that men can identify with and relate easier to the primate gorilla, more than he can with women.

It is interesting to note that men have more similarities with the gorilla than they do with women. Men and gorillas have a lot in common. They both are hairy, have dense muscle fiber, heavy bones, and both have a humerus bone [which is located between the crazy bone (elbow) and the thinking bone (brain)].

Some say, ". . . *a way to a man's [gorilla's] heart is through his stomach,*" it doesn't matter much what it is, so long as there is plenty of it.

Men and gorillas have less acute senses than women [some women say no sense at all]: Such as sight, hearing, taste, color perception, and smell [sometimes smelling a bit too strong].

Men and gorillas have thick skin with fewer nerve endings [therefore having less feelings than women]. Men and gorillas also focus on one thing at a time [which drives women crazy].

So, what's the difference between men and gorillas, not much say some women. Some women lay claim that men have the same large head, small beady eyes, and similar intellect as the ape. Some women state that men grunt, mumble, carry on, and walk like apes. It's just a matter of perception.

Men and gorillas were created to be fast runners and good climbers, assisting them in being a good bread-winner and a defender of territory and property.

Women, on the other hand, have very acute senses. They have soft skin, with many nerve endings [lots of feelings]. They can focus on many things at the same time [which confuses men]. They talk very soft [except when they are angry]. They have exceptional hearing [hearing a bit too much at times]. They talk a lot [men say in one minute what they did in eight hours, while women may take an hour to explain what they did in eight minutes].

Women were constructed to have babies; to gather fruits and nuts; and are sometimes uncontrollably emotional [which confuses men and women].

Yes, these comments were written by a man, with tongue-in-cheek and with a play on words. But, whether you like it or not, it is a basic perception as viewed by many men and women.

There is a lot of truth here, it is just that we don't understand or correctly perceive the underlying meaning of the differences between men and women.

So, what's the difference between men and women?

RECEPTION AND PERCEPTION

Physical reception refers to the way in which we receive, sort, store and retrieve biological information [see, touch, hear, smell, taste].

Mental perception relates to how we interpret the information that we receive, which is determined by relativity.

The determination of how we draw conclusions from, act upon, or react to various information is relative to ourselves. This is mainly influenced by parents, teachers, relatives, peers, and from our experiences. All of which influences our values and beliefs.

Since the reception and perception of men and women are quite different, their conclusions and attitudes towards each other's actions and reactions are equally as different, which is the basis for the misunderstandings and disagreements between the sexes.

A man and his wife had worked very hard one morning [him doing yard work and her doing house work] both doing tiring and routine chores.

They both finished their chores at about the same time. The husband, after using up all of his allotted energy doing his chores, lies down to become a couch potato, watching his favorite sport on television. His wife, while resting as she talks on the telephone, leans over and says, *"Dear, let's go for a long drive to relax."* After a moment of silence, [now this really confuses him, how can she talk on the phone, read a novel, rest, and talk to him at the same time, when he can barely keep his mind on the TV? Also, how can she have so much energy left over]. Finally he replies [not being sure if she's serious because she's talking on the phone to someone else] with an undecipherable moan, *"OK dear, let's go."*

So off they go. They're driving down the road [he's focusing on the road, while she's settling in, trying to get comfortable].

The wife decides to roll down the window to let the cold fresh air in because she's too hot [naturally he's freezing] the wife then pulls out a pocket novel to read. While reading, she takes out her nail polish to do some touch up work on her nails. Then the wife turns and says, *"Dear, would you turn the radio up and play my favorite station, I can't do it until my nails dry?"* [He was hoping for a more relaxing station, she likes hard rock]. The husband reaches over to turn the radio up, and the car swerves a little. The wife snaps back! *"Will you keep your mind on the road!"*

She now tries to start a conversation because her husband has been too quiet, and says, *"Look, Honey, at how pretty the flowers are on the side of the cliff below us."* As he tries to respond to her request, she exclaims! *"Look out! There's a car in front of us and by the way you just missed our turn off!"*

At this point, as you could well imagine, he's not a very happy camper, becoming more and more frustrated and very confused. And she's becoming very nervous and agitated [at his inability to keep the car under control]. The stress mounts! How will it end? Is it *"Damsel in stress, or damn, he's losing his mind"?*

Let us take a closer look at our scenario. What we will find is that: **HOW** we perceive is based upon our own values and beliefs [which are quite different between men and women]; and **WHAT** we perceive is a lack of courtesy [understanding].

The injustice is that we blame others for our misunderstandings [lack of courtesy] then we retaliate with anger. Let us identify each potential problem and see if we can unravel the great mystery of the sexes.

Men live in a man's world and women live in a women's world, and both relate from that point of view. For example, a man at work slaps a woman on her backside, and says, *"How're doin' buddy?"* After picking herself up [being in pain and with bruises] gulps, *"I'm fine, I think"* [not knowing whether she has been insulted or complimented].

The man was living in his perceived world, and as such, was giving that women a loving gesture, just as if she were a man. But not giving due consideration to the fact that she might bruise and be more fragile than he. This was a natural act for a man [natural doesn't mean correct].

Now, getting back to our story. Women need to realize that men allocate a specific amount of energy to each task that they wish to perform, and when that energy is used up, they need to rest until it is replenished. It is also very important to note that women must give as much advance warning as possible so that the man can set aside sufficient energy for an assigned task or activity.

Men, on the other hand, might consider reserving extra energy for that one more honey-due that she forgot or was saving for just the right moment [Guys, this is the moment that you can really shine, be prepared]. Women need to understand that when a man needs to rest, this means absence of thought, effort, and concentration [decision making and conversation is a big No-No during his rest time].

Women have a ready reserve energy bank, called fat cells, which allows them to have more endurance than men [the only time when this appears not to be true is at bedtime, when she suddenly becomes very tired and like magic, headaches appear].

Men have very efficient sweat glands, which is instrumental in controlling their body temperature for [fight or flight] keeping them cool. Women are just the opposite. So the man might consider taking a jacket along so as to not make the other uncomfortable by turning up the heat or by freezing the other by rolling down the window, letting the cold air in.

The ability to focus, receive, sort, and retrieve information is more of a biological function than what most would think. Men have fewer connectors between their right brain and their left brain, than women.

Women have more right and left brain connectors, therefore, receive 40% more information than men. They also have a better mental sorting system and retrieve information faster. This is one of the reasons why women can do so many things at the same time, and why men can only focus on one thing at a time. So, women don't be so harsh on men [don't judge them by your capabilities] when he has difficulty chewing gum, walking, and talking at the same time [he has a biological excuse].

Have any of you women ever felt that men were not interested in what you had to say, gave you a strange response to a question, or not answered you at all? The answer may be quite simple. He either did not hear what you had said or he did not understand what you had said.

Men have less hearing ability than women. Most men have lost the ability to hear high frequencies or tones, making it difficult for them to understand what women say.

Now, let us return to our couple taking their long drive. We have learned so far that men have hearing difficulties and focus on one thing at a time.

Let us look at their communication dilemma. The husband is focusing on his driving, attempting to get from Point-A to Point-B. He's cold because the window is rolled down, which also is adding a lot of background noise. The radio is turned up, not his relaxing music either, which is adding more confusion.

Coupled with the fact that he doesn't hear very well, and his wife now wants him to look at the flowers on the side of the cliff below them, it's a miracle that he kept the car on the road at all, let alone carry on a conversation.

Have any of you women ever noticed a man, while driving in a car, turn his head toward you when you were talking? He was attempting to read your lips so that he could understand what you were saying. And yet, you cussed him out for not keeping his eyes on the road. Women should try speaking slower, clearer and loud enough to be heard by a man.

The lesson that needs to be learned here is that men and women need to communicate well, both need to express their needs and desires, as well as expressing their shortcomings for better understanding. Take the time to understand the needs of those around you, and communicate with passion.

Chapter 8
Understanding Relationships

BE HONEST

It is meaningful to acquire knowledge, but it is misleading to expect knowledge alone to bring peace, joy, and love. Love is understanding, which comes from within ourselves.

We tell ourselves, *"If I could only find the right person to love, then I would be happy!"* So we search for someone for whom our emotions tell us is the right person, and we experience some pleasurable moments.

But since most of us do not know how to love unconditionally, our relationships gradually deteriorate. Then we decide that we did not find that right person after all. So we go on searching for another and another, until we become so exhausted that we either give up looking or we settle for someone less than desired. As we grow, we discover that it is far more important to be the right person, than to find the right person.

Our negative emotions are simply the result of an extensive pattern of fears that we have experienced and from the scars left behind from those experiences. These emotional wounds lead us to perceive differences that misdirect our thinking process, instead of allowing us to seek the good and to seek the positive that enables us to understand and to love others.

Unfortunately, most of us have not been taught how to love unconditionally. Almost all of our loving has been motivated by emotional desires, programmed into us at an early age. Most of our love experiences have taught us that love must be earned or deserved before we can accept or give it. This is called conditional love or negative love. It is no wonder then, that our well-meaning but unfruitful attempts to love usually ends up in alienation or in separation.

We have been taught to place conditions on our love. We say, *"If you really love me, you would . . ."* This is an example of conditional love that is manipulative and controlling, which must be avoided and never used.

True love is simply accepting others without criticism, discovering their perfection, and giving without conditions.

Before learning to love others, we must first learn to love ourselves. We need to feel that no matter how poorly we have judged our past actions to be, each day our life begins anew; canceling the past, making way for the future. We must learn to forgive our past.

*Return to him
your purest love,
and he will cease
from doing wrong;
for love will
purify the heart
of him who is loved
as truly as it
purifies the heart
of him who loves.*

RELATIONSHIPS by Dr. Isolde "Miriamme" Czukor

"Relationships are difficult at best, and we deceive ourselves when we circumvent the truth. We weave our fruitless, vain scenarios with plots that we have conjured up from glamour and illusion. No matter that the map we choose to follow does not conform to territory. We blame the object of our sad contrivances, and then tell all and sundry we are disappointed. And to that one we once had held so dear, we say, 'How could you . . . ? You're not the person that I thought you were.' When in fact, they are the very same. They have not changed one jot. 'Twas we who made them up out of whole cloth to suit our own specific and periled needs. We hide our eyes from truth and point the finger of our scorn at them. Why can't we love them as they really are, and learn to bear and then forbear again, because we really love? Oh, how the world would change if we would take the blinders off our eyes. Wrap not only those we love but whom all we meet with the light of courtesy and understanding, and respecting their integrity."

Chapter 9

Rekindling Marriage

NEED A SPARK?

Before placing that sparkle into your relationship, a basic code of conduct is required and must be agreed to [for open and honest communication] for a meaningful and everlasting relationship to exist.

I Thou shalt allow thy partner the right to express what he or she feels or thinks without condemnation.

II Thou shalt allow thy partner the right to tell the truth without disbelief and without reprisal.

III Thou shalt allow thy partner the right to be trusted and to be believed without interrogation.

IV Thou shalt allow thy partner the right to be listened to and to be understood without interruption.

V Thou shalt allow thy partner the right to admit weakness without ridicule or shame.

VI Thou shalt allow thy partner the right to be heard in the context of the moment without bringing forth the past.

VIII Thou shalt allow thy partner the right to grow and to expand their awareness without impedance.

IX Thou shalt allow thy partner the right to seek help, friendship, and support without permission.

X Thou shalt allow thy partner the right to be forgiven without conditions.

Even though a husband and wife may seem to be model partners, their marriage may still have problems. All it may need is a little rekindling by putting that spark of life back into it.

Some pitfalls of married life are not spending enough quality time together and not having enough fun. Whole evenings may pass in silence or in separation. Even sex may have lost its sparkle. This marriage could be summed up in one word . . . dull. Replacing boredom with affection and with humor is the answer.

Externally, everything may look fine in this relationship. Yet something has slipped away, and no one is even aware that it has gone. That something is fun, and it disappears not by decision but by default.

The spirit of fun is crucial for a fulfilling relationship to exist. Couples who have fun together are really saying, *"I trust you to love me even when I'm being silly."*

The joy of marriage is easy to lose in today's worried-hurried world, but it can be brought back if both partners are willing to commit. It does not require a great deal of time or effort, just commitment.

If your relationship has lost its flame, here are some sparks to rekindle it.

LET YOUR GUARD DOWN. Too many couples consider marriage a deadly serious matter, a cheerless routine of payments, meetings, chores, and other duties. They have been told so frequently to work at marriage that they lose the enjoyment of having fun, ultimately dissolving the relationship.

Some couples feel guilty about having a good time with so many seemingly important duties to perform. They put the children first, without thinking that the children will suffer most if the core of the marriage is not in harmony.

All work and no play will make for a very dull relationship. So, the first step in lighting that flame in your relationship is to grant yourselves permission to have fun.

PLAN TO BE SPONTANEOUS. Planned spontaneity sounds contradictory, but you cannot be spontaneous if you do not allow the time. Carve time for yourselves, away from other distractions, to do whatever that gives the both of you pleasure.

Take an afternoon or a weekend, just the two of you. Go for a long drive, or go for a walk in the park. Hold hands, walk on the grass, act silly if you choose. You might spend a weekend away from home [without even leaving town]. A nice hotel within your own hometown can be just as romantic as one a thousand miles away.

Some more examples of sharing and giving (having fun) might be to set aside an evening a week to date each other. One might hire a baby-sitter, surprising the other as to what will be in store for the evening. You might go dancing, another time to a concert, maybe one time just a stroll on the beach. One evening you might create a romantic candlelight dinner at home. The point is not where you go or what you do, it is the message that time was reserved just for the two of you.

BE PLAYFUL. Remember how you used to call each other pet names? Or giggle for no reason, just because you were happy together?

Yet playfulness is often the first casualty in marriage. After couples get married, they sometimes say to themselves, Grow up! Act your age! But playful intimacy is something that transcends age.

Above all, intimate play is a matter of reinforcing a relationship by touching. The affectionate pat, the sudden hug, the teasing tickle may say, *"I love being with you"* more effectively than words.

I love you when you're teasing.

I love when you're bad.

I love when you're pleasing.

I love when you're mad.

I love you when you're sneezing.

I love you when you're sad.

I love you when you're smiling.

I love you when you're glad.

But the real reason I love you,

Is just because you're you.

SURPRISE EACH OTHER. Doing something unexpected for your spouse shows that you have been thinking of him or her. A surprise says, *"You have been in my thoughts even while we were apart."*

One thoughtful surprise might be to pluck a flower from your garden and place it by your spouse's bedside or set an intimate card on the breakfast table.

LAUGH TOGETHER. Many couples once laughed together frequently, but rarely do so anymore. Yet there are ways to recharge your relationship with amusement. One spouse could make an effort to remember the jokes or quips that were amusing at work so that they could be retold later, while the other spouse might tape cartoons to the refrigerator. Couples with DVD's might rent comedies to laugh at together.

A shared joke draws couples closer, and says, *"I know you well enough to understand what makes you laugh."* Couples who laugh at the same jokes are more likely to remain together. A common sense-of-humor reflects shared values.

BRING JOY TO YOUR SEX LIFE. Of all aspects of married life, sex is most likely to fall into a predictable routine. It is also the area most difficult to change.

Variety is the spice of sex. Why must sex be limited to the 11th hour of the night? Why not early morning? Why not weekend afternoons?

Good sex does not always start in the bedroom. Dining, massaging, and cozy remarks all carry sexual overtones and will heighten your pleasure.

A couple may find that by showering together or by massaging each other is an exciting prelude to sex. Another couple may send the kids to Grandma's and then snuggle down before a roaring fire and make love.

Too often couples concentrate on the act of intercourse itself and ignore other ways of giving pleasure. For most women cuddling and closeness may be most important of all.

Most marriages thrive on the sunlight of familiarity and routine, but the water of novelty and spontaneity is needed to keep the relationship from withering. Couples who laughed together once must not allow joylessness to overtake their marriage. Fun is important. Successful marriages have an atmosphere of lightheartedness.

Be affectionate, laugh, and communicate with each other. Add that spark of life and rediscover the love and the beauty of your marriage.

Follow your dreams
wherever you go,
don't be distracted
by less worthy a goal.

Nourish your dreams
help them to grow,
let your heart hold them
love sparking a glow.

Follow your dreams
pursue them with haste,
time is too precious
too fleeing to waste.

Be faithful and loyal
all your life through,
the dreams you follow
will start to come true.

Chapter 10
A Sensual Relationship

HOW EXCITING

KEYS TO A SENSUAL VIBRANT RELATIONSHIP

HONESTY IS THE BEST POLICY. You slam the door on the possibility of a meaningful relationship by lying, pretending, withholding, or blaming. If you are faking sexual gratification, or you are attempting to please your partner by telling them what you think they want to hear, you are on the wrong track. Attempting to preserve emotional status quo is an insidious trap that many of us fall into. Rather than doing anything that will rock the relationship, many of us hold onto patterns that are routine and boring. Lovemaking, vacations, and dinner table conversations become predictable and tiresome.

If you think that you are pleasing your partner by not saying what you want, how you feel, or telling your partner what you think they want to hear, you are making a mistake. At the heart of true intimacy is truth.

PLAN FOR QUALITY TIME. We live in an enormously stressful world where everyone is hurried and worried, and if the moment comes to let the day's worries dissolve, the majority of us do so by watching television instead of talking with each other in a loving, intimate way. Many people spend more time wishing or day dreaming about an exciting relationship instead of cultivating one.

It cannot be said often enough that making love requires time. Spontaneity is a terrific turn-on, but given the realities of the average household, it is clear that planning for lovemaking is almost a necessity. Experts say that by taking the time to plan a romantic rendezvous will actually kindle sexuality. Planned lovemaking is something to look forward to.

HAVE A COMMITMENT TO SEXUALITY. In plain language, this means accepting yourself as a sensual being who enjoys giving and receiving pleasure. It is surprising to note how many of us will not allow ourselves to think, feel, or act this way. Be free to love with passion.

Convey to your partner that you are truly interested in them. Many of us feel that our partner is lukewarm or too inhibited about lovemaking. Being truly interested means completely enjoying your own natural, healthy sexuality. For one person, this might mean recognizing their impulses for lovemaking instead of subduing them or feeling guilty. For another it might mean summoning the courage to discuss sexual problems or allowing one's self to explore sexual fantasies with their partner.

Some people are born with the *golden-touch*. They have within themselves an intuitive understanding of sensuality. They know how to set the mood, dress, touch, move, etc.

Those not born with the *golden-touch* must learn to develop their own emotional responses to giving and receiving pleasure.

Think about cooking for a minute. Without looking at a cook book, the born cook instinctively knows how to put a meal together. Others have to follow recipes and measure out all the ingredients carefully. Both methods work. You can learn to be sensual. You must learn to convey what you desire and what you need, to inspire pleasure to both you and your partner.

INSIST ON GOOD COMMUNICATION. Perhaps the most important tool you have in sustaining a meaningful relationship is communication. You can have a silent, meaningless relationship where conflicts are avoided, but a relationship with substance is one in which problems are faced, discussed, and resolved.

If you express what you really need and desire, without fear or shame, then your needs will be met with surprising quickness. When fears of failure or rejection are expressed openly, they will lose their power to hurt. *"I'm afraid you'll leave me if I say what I really want,"* or *"I feel vulnerable and exposed when I do that,"* are surprisingly countered with, *"I didn't know that you felt that way."*

Unless you tell your partner how you feel and what you want, how are they to know? One of the greatest problems between two people lies in the assumption that their partner should automatically sense what you want or do not want. Almost nothing could be further from the truth. This falls within the realm of Mind Reading or ESP. Attempting to be an effective lover without conventional communication is like learning target shooting blindfolded.

Countless physical and emotional feelings occur when you make love. You can become sensitive to these changes by carefully observing your partner's physical responses and by revealing your own reactions to various touches and movements. Simple phrases that begin with, *"I like that,"* or *"It feels so good when . . ."* gives your partner a clearer understanding of what you desire.

OVERCOME YOUR FEARS. For many of us, fear is a well-known bedfellow, and it is these fears that are some of the greatest inhibitors of lovemaking. Most men would be surprised to know how many women are embarrassed about their bodies. Women worry about their waists, thighs, etc. In short, one of the greatest sexual fears among women is the fear of not being desirable enough. Men, on the other hand, fear not being large enough, therefore not successfully satisfying their partner. You can overcome these fears by engaging in an intimate [open and honest] conversation.

Many couples make love with the lights off or with their pajamas or nightgowns on because they are concerned about how they look. We all appreciate perfectly beautiful faces and bodies, but it should be obvious that most of us have to live with our seemingly imperfect selves. Feeling comfortable with your own body is a prerequisite to feeling comfortable with someone else's body.

Many women also worry that if they take the initiative, their partner will consider them too aggressive and not feminine enough, being concerned that their partner will perceive this as a direct hit on a traditionally masculine role.

Most men prefer that their partner take the initiative some of the time. A woman who says, *"I feel like seducing you tonight"* is far likelier to get a warm reception than the one who demands unsolicited action.

You may be tempted to say, *"But I know these things."* It is true that much of what is here is just common sense. Yet, when was the last time that you served your mate breakfast in bed? When was the last time that you took a walk in a park together? When was the last time that you gave your mate a good massage, if ever? When was the last time that you talked late into the night? When was the last time that you just held hands with your mate, or said, *"I love you."*

If there is one message that comes through from couples who have made something very special of their lives together, it is this: Set aside the time to understand each other and talk about the things that will make your relationship work . . . and then do them!

I love your humor without ridicule
I love your honesty without deceit
I love your passion without pretense
I love your understanding without doubt

I love you creatively without conditioning
I love you physically without pretending
I love you freely without restriction
I love you now without reservation

Chapter 11
Being Single

OR MARRIED?

Have you been looking for your Cinderella or your Prince Charming but found only witches or frogs? Are you choosing the wrong mate, or are they all emotional cripples?

Are you looking for that special someone who will appreciate you, support you, build your castle or make you King or Queen? The older we get the more it appears that this special person is just a fantasy.

There may be no right person, and maybe you should give up this fantasy and get on with your life before it is too late. Where the confusion lies is that you need to be the right person before you can find the right person.

There may be more advantages to being single than being married to a non-fulfilling mate. But to hear the tales of woe from the singles population, one would not think so. Single men and women talk of loneliness, financial problems, and dissatisfactions with life, but so do married couples. These problems may not be resolved by having a mate.

Singles who are unhappy are in a state of waiting. They are waiting to buy a house, waiting to find a career, or waiting to create the lifestyle that they want. They are not getting on with their life because they are waiting for a mate.

These single men and women fear that by the time they get their lives in order, they will be too set in their ways to find a lasting and meaningful relationship. This is not true. On the contrary, a single person who has put his or her life in order is happier and is more attractive to the opposite sex. Healthy, happy relationships will happen only between *"two healthy happy individuals."*

Besides, when you learn to be happy as a single, you may not want to marry. After all, the grass is not always greener on the other side of the matrimonial fence. Just ask your married friends, for they may tell you that marriage does not guarantee a constant lifetime of companionship. Often one partner becomes overly involved in work or overly involved with children inhibiting companionship with their mate.

Married couples may also tell you that marriage is no guarantee of a great sex life. Couples often grow bored or angry with each other and may not have sex for long periods of time. Others use the bedroom as a battleground (or as a weapon to control another by allowing or withholding sex) instead of a haven for love.

Partners are not always supportive of financial or career goals. They may become jealous and drain you of your energy. In marriage, you may react to what you believe are the needs of your mate, rather than acting in your own best interest.

As a single, you are more likely to follow your career goals. You do not need to worry about how a drop in income or a change to a new location will affect your mate.

Contrary to popular belief among singles, marriage is no guarantee against loneliness. You can be lonelier lying in bed next to your mate who is being non-attentive, than curled up in bed alone reading a good book.

Married men and women will often wait and hope that their mate will be more intimate, ultimately blaming their mate for their loneliness.

Couples will often limit themselves to each other's relationship. Singles, on the other hand, have more choices in satisfying their needs. They can call lovers or friends, or choose to meet someone new, without having to defend those relationships.

A person who is single has less pressure to conform to the expectations of others. It is easier to be you. You can take personal risks that you might otherwise be afraid to take if you were worried about the expectations of a mate. You can stay up all night, act silly, or take your credit cards over the limit if you choose.

Take your life off of hold and stop waiting. Get on with your life and become a healthier person.

Remember this: You will not be any happier in marriage right now than you are at this very moment being single [your happiness comes from within you].

TODAY IS MY DAY

Today I shall remind myself that I can do anything
that I choose to focus on; morning, noon, or evening.

Today belongs to me to do with as I choose,
with faith in me, I know I shall not lose.

Today I choose to feel wonderful and exciting,
and I know that life will be fun and igniting.

Today I expect new ideas and opportunities
to flow unto me like a mid-summer's breeze.

Today I know that I will enhance my well-being,
happiness, and prosperity, far beyond engineering.

Today I will be more loving, more accepting
[of myself and others], and less interrupting.

Today I know that the energy of expressing myself
is energy that brings joy from heaven's open shelf.

Chapter 12
Friendship and Friends

IT'S UP TO YOU

While you are deciding what to do with your life, why not meet new friends and re-acquaint yourself with friends lost.

Friends make wonderful companions. They will comfort you when you are ill or lost. They are someone that you will consider feeling safe confiding in with your deepest secrets or personal problems. They are also someone that you can share exciting times or victories.

Friends are a great resource for new activities, networking, or adventures, such as creative cooking, travel, job referrals, or leisure time activities. The only limit is your imagination.

Friends are terrific sounding boards when you need someone to share new ideas or need input on special matters or problems.

Friends are enjoyable, such as when sharing walks or talks, exercising or sports, window shopping or dining. The sky's the limit.

Friends are found everywhere, but the best way to find a friend is to be a friend. Helping and sharing with others is very rewarding: Adding your light of courtesy and thoughtfulness to others will brighten the glow of this planet called Earth.

The key points of friendship are; to be discreet, honest, thoughtful, and a good listener. Remember, don't be just a giver or a taker, share with passion.

Instead of moping around feeling sorry for yourself, find [and be] a friend, and share your life with passion.

Let us be the first to give a friendly sign,
to nod first, smile first, speak first, and
if such a thing is necessary, forgive first.

He who sows seeds of courtesy will reap friendship and he who plants flowers of kindness will gather Love.

Friendship can only be purchased with friendship. A friend is one who comes to you when all others leave.

The light of friendship is like the glow of a star, at night it can be seen when all around is dark.

Friendship is building bridges, and not building walls. Do not judge a friend until you stand in his place.

The only way to get a friend is to be a friend, and the only way to keep a friend is to act like a friend.

A friend is a person with whom you dare to be yourself, they know all about you, and yet they still love you.

To handle yourself, use your head and think within. To handle friends, use your heart and express aloud.

A friend is a present that you give yourself, and a stranger is just a friend that you have not yet met.

Friends are made from many acts and lost from only one. Praise your friends openly, reprimand them in private.

The only safe and sure way to destroy an enemy is to make him your friend, and your friend's friend as well.

Always speak the truth and you will never be concerned with your memory, or losing your true friends.

Your friend has a friend and your friend's friend has a friend . . .

BE DISCREET! DISCREET! DISCREET! DISCREET!

Chapter 13
Being Healthy and Happy

MIND OR MATTER?

Being healthy and happy is a natural state, and the means for achieving it is within the grasp of each of us. A judicious mixture of clear thinking, humor, self-confidence, and love are the ingredients for productive and joyous living. There are two main qualities that are involved in productive living.

The first quality involves the ability to correctly identify and to choose your emotions. Begin to examine your life in the light of the choices you have made or have failed to make. This places the responsibility of what you are and how you feel, on you. You are the sum total of your choices. With an appropriate amount of motivation and effort, you can do [or be] anything that you make your mind up to.

IF YOU CAN IMAGINE IT, YOU CAN ACHIEVE IT
IF YOU CAN DREAM IT, YOU CAN BECOME IT

The second quality is fulfilled through taking charge of the present. It is an essential part of eliminating negative behavior and creating happiness. There is only one moment that you will experience anything, and that is NOW, the present moment. Yet, a great deal of time is wasted by dwelling on the past and on the future.

TODAY'S BEAUTIFUL MOMENTS ARE
TOMORROW'S BEAUTIFUL MEMORIES

Ask yourself, *"Should I avoid doing the things that I really want? Should I live my life as others want? Are things important to accumulate? Is putting-things-off the way to live?"* Chances are that your rebuttal can be summed up in a few words; live, be you, enjoy, and love with passion.

A meaningful and joyful life is living each moment of every day, being healthy, happy, and free of fear. If you live each day for all that it is worth and live without fear, then you will be a productive and joyful person.

Productive people do not have emotional crises because they are in charge of their lives. They know how to choose happiness over depression because they know how to deal with the problems within their lives. Rather than measuring their effectiveness by their ability to solve problems, they measure it by their capacity for maintaining themselves as happy and worthwhile individuals, regardless of whether their problems get resolved or not.

Feelings and emotions are reactions that you choose. If you are in charge of your feelings and emotions, then you will not create self-defeating reactions. Once you have learned that you can feel what you choose, then you will be on the road towards a more productive life. Consider a given emotion as a choice, rather than as a condition of life. This is the very heart and soul of personal freedom, and of a healthy happy life.

Here is a logical approach for taking charge of your emotional world: You can control your thoughts; your feelings come from your thoughts; therefore, you can control your feelings.

You have the power to think whatever you choose to allow into your mind. Your thoughts are your own, uniquely yours to keep, to change, to shape, to put on hold, or to discard.

Your emotions are a physical reaction or expression to your thoughts. Every emotion that you have was preceded by a thought. If you control your thoughts, and your emotions come from your thoughts, then you can control your emotions.

You are responsible for how you feel. If you feel what you think, then you can learn to think differently, changing your negative feelings into positive ones.

Taking charge of your life begins with awareness. Catch yourself when you say things like, *"That person hurt my feelings."* Recall what you were thinking at the time. You should have said something like, *"I allowed that person to hurt my feelings."* This places the control and responsibility of your feelings upon yourself where it belongs.

A thought becomes a belief when you accept it from the heart and having enough faith in that thought that it will manifest itself in your world.

You can choose to make any experience enjoyable and exciting. It is up to you to take control of your thoughts, then practice feeling and behaving the way in which you desire.

Virtually all negative emotions will result in some form of helplessness, and this alone is a solid reason for eliminating negative emotions from your life.

One way to control helplessness, however slight, is learning to live in the present. Present moment living is at the heart of productive living. When you think about it, there really is no other moment that you can live in or that you can have control over. NOW is all there is. The past is gone forever, and the future is just another present moment to live in when it arrives. One thing is certain, you cannot relive the past, nor can you live the future until it appears.

Wishing, hoping, and regretting are the most dangerous tactics for avoiding the present. As you look back on your life, you will find that you have rarely regretted something that you had done. It is what you had failed to do that is tormenting.

Develop an appreciation for the present. Value your present moments. Using them in any self-defeating manner means that you have wasted that time and that energy forever.

You are not a victim of circumstance, for the situations that you are involved in were created from your thoughts. People blame circumstances for what happens to them. Individuals who get along in this world are the individuals who envision the situations that they want, setting in motion the required thoughts to find or to create the situations that they desire.

Love is the ability and the willingness to allow those you care for to be what they choose, without any insistence that they satisfy you.

How can you reach that point of being able to let others be what they choose, without insisting that they meet your expectations? BY LOVING YOURSELF. By believing that you are a worthy person. Once you accept yourself as a worthy person, you will not need others to reinforce your values by making their behavior conform to your dictates.

Once you truly love yourself, you are then able to love others, and to give to others. Now you can give to others because of the genuine pleasure that you receive from being a helper or a lover.

If you cannot give love, then neither can you receive love. Self-love means accepting yourself just the way you are. You are a worthy person because you are a decent and deserving person, and you choose to see yourself that way. Acceptance means absence of criticism, and recognizing your perfection.

Criticizing others accomplishes nothing. Neither does permitting others to abuse you with their criticism. A simple question generally ends this useless and unpleasant behavior of others, *"Why are you telling me this?"*

Being able to accept yourself without complaint involves an understanding of both self-love and the complaint-process. If you genuinely love yourself, then complaining to others, who can do little to help, becomes absurdly impossible to defend. And if you notice behavior in yourself or in others that you dislike, rather than complaining, actively set about creating the necessary corrective action. With your mind now working for you rather than against you, self-love activities are on the horizon.

The following measures will help you to build your sense of self-esteem based upon your own worth. Select new responses to others who attempt to reach you with love or with acceptance. Rather than instantly being skeptical of a loving gesture, accept it with a *"Thank you"* or *"I'm happy that you feel that way."* If you are shy, go out of your way to meet someone new. If there is someone whom you feel genuine love towards, say it out rightly, *"I love you."* While you check out their reactions, pat yourself on the back for taking the risk.

Eliminate jealousy by recognizing that it is a put-down on yourself. By comparing yourself to others, imagining that you are less worthy, you make others more important than yourself. Someone can always choose another without it being a reflection on you. It is their value system that is in question not your worthiness.

With practice, any situation, perhaps the one in which you had found yourself to be jealous in, can be reversed. You need to believe so much in yourself that you need neither love nor approval from others to give yourself value.

If you perceive yourself to be unhappy at this very moment, just think how sad you would feel if you lost everything that you have right now, and how happy you would feel, if it was all returned. It's all relative.

We know what is best for us,
so why should we complain.
We always want the sun to shine,
but know there must be rain.

We love to hear laughter and glee
and the merriment of cheer.
But our hearts would lose their tenderness
if we never shed a tear.

The world is always testing us
with suffering and sorrow.
It tests us, not to punish us,
but to help us meet tomorrow.

For growing trees are strengthened more
when withstanding the tempest storm,
and the sharpest cut of the chisel
gives the marble true grace and form.

So when we are troubled and low,
and everything seems to go wrong,
just look around and see the beauty,
for it is love that keeps us strong.

Chapter 14
Approval Seeking

BE YOUR OWN HERO

Approval seeking is negative behavior when it becomes a need rather than a want. The need for approval seeking must be eliminated from your life if you desire personal fulfillment. When someone disapproves of something that you have said or done, instead of feeling hurt, remind yourself that you have just run into one of those folks in the 50% bracket who will not agree with you. Being aware that you will meet with some disapproval of whatever you say or do is the way out of the tunnel of despair.

Thank someone for providing you with information that you disliked or disagreed with. This will put an end to approval seeking, and end any further negative discussion. Others have a right to be the way they are and it really has nothing to do with you.

Check yourself on the extent to which you are chained to your past. All self-defeating statements are based upon the use of four neurotic phrases:

"That's me," "I've always been that way," "I can't help it," and *"That's my nature."* These are the inhibitors that prevent you from growing, from changing, and from making your life fresh, exciting, and heaped with everlasting fulfillment.

If you are genuinely satisfied with any of these neurotic phrases then let them be. But if you will admit to any of these negative phrases getting in your way of enjoying a fulfilled life, then it is time to make some changes.

The excuse for hanging onto your past by using these negative phrases can neatly be summed up in one word . . . avoidance. Whenever you choose to dodge a certain activity or gloss over a personality defect, you will justify your behavior with a self-defeating statement.

In fact, after you use these phrases long enough, you will begin to believe them yourself, and at that moment you will become a finished product destined to remain as you are for the rest of your days.

The use of negative phrases enables you to avoid facing your fears and the risk of exposing them. They dramatize behavior that cause these neurotic terms to be carried out. To eliminate these negative phrases, avoid using them whenever possible. Substitute negative phrases with sentences like, *"Until today I've chosen to be that way,"* or *"I used to label myself . . ."*

Pledge yourself to eliminate all self-defeating statements by writing down that commitment on paper and placing it in a prominent place. Let others know of your commitment. After deciding which statements that you need to eliminate, ask your friends to remind you whenever you use them.

Set behavioral goals to act differently from your past. For example, if you consider yourself to be shy, introduce yourself to someone new whom you would otherwise have avoided, or talk with a trusted friend who will help you to combat your negative behavior.

Ask a friend to signal you each time that you use one of your *"I am"* traps. The signal might be a subtle pat on the shoulder or a nod of the head. Just the two of you will know and understand the signal and what it means.

Watch out for your neurotic phrases. Whenever you notice, them, correct yourself out loud. Change: *"That's me,"* to *"That was me,"* or *"I can't help it,"* to *"I can change,"* or *"I've always been that way,"* to *"I used to be that way,"* or *"That's my nature,"* to *"That's what I believed was my nature, and now I have dominion over my being."*

Look within your being
listen to your heart.
You can reach your goals
and fulfill your dreams;
by making your fears depart.

YOU CAN DO IT!

You can make it happen now
a fresh and exciting reality.
By not accepting fear,
the way it was and used to be;
the dark side of negativity.

YOU CAN DO IT!

Nothing can hold you back
except the fears you hold within.
They were created by you, and
now you can say to them good-bye;
applying commitment and discipline.

YOU CAN DO IT!

Declare it to yourself
believe it in your heart.
"Let fear go, set it free"
Make everyday a new beginning
with a joyous and positive start.

YOU CAN DO IT!

EACH DAY ELIMINATE A NEGATIVE PHRASE. If you do not like your stubborn *"I am"* traps, then give yourself a relief and rid yourself of one *"I am"* a day. All of your *"I am's"* are learned avoidance patterns, and you can relearn anything if you make the commitment to do so.

There is no such thing as human nature. The term is designed to pigeonhole people, and to create excuses. You are the sum product of your choices. Every *"I am"* that you treasure must be relabeled, *"I've chosen to be that way."* Those old, tiresome labels prevent you from living a productive and joyous life.

Chapter 15

Letting go of Fear

GUILT/WORRY

Guilt is a state of feeling pain resulting from a belief that you have behaved wrongly or immorally, while worry is a state of feeling troubled or uneasy.

Both guilt and worry will inhibit you from effectively living in the present. Feeling guilty is being helpless in the present as a result of a fear that developed in your past. While worry is the contrivance that keeps you helpless in the present over a fear concerning the future. Unfortunately, you do not have control over the past or over the future, only over the present. You might visualize this by projecting feelings of worry concerning an event that has yet to occur or by projecting feelings of guilt concerning an event that has already happened.

It is not the experiences of today that drives you mad but the remorse over something that occurred yesterday or the dread of what tomorrow may disclose.

Feeling guilty and worrying are a waste of time and energy, especially since they are connected with situations that are beyond your control. So why not utilize your precious time and energy to enjoy life; *"Being productive in the present, rather than feeling guilty about the past or worrying about the future."*

GUILT

Guilt is one of the most useless of all negative states of mind. It is by far one of the greatest misuses of emotional energy. Why? Because we feel helpless in the present over something that has already taken place, and no amount of feeling guilty will ever change history.

You experience pain from the feeling of guilt resulting from a seemingly wrongful decision in your past. It will prevent you from making meaningful decisions in the present and will drain you of energy.

Avoiding the repetition of negative behavior or of your past mistakes is healthy, and a necessary part of growth. But feeling guilty [being hurt, upset, or helpless about a historical event] is misusing your energy in the present. Feeling guilty is futile as well as unhealthy, and no amount of feeling guilty will ever undo anything.

The *"If you love me"* phrase is one way of manipulating others by using guilt. This tactic is widely used when one wants to punish another for some specific behavior. Whenever someone does not measure up, guilt will be applied to get that person back into line. The slighted one must feel guilty for not having loved or treated the other in a certain manner. Rubbish, pure rubbish! This is commonly known as the *"guilt-trip."*

Begin to view the past as something that will never be undone, no matter how strongly you feel about it. It is over, and any guilt that you may choose will not change the past, nor will it help you or anyone else.

Ask yourself, *"What am I avoiding in the present by feeling guilty about the past."* By eliminating that particular excuse, you will reduce your need for feeling guilty.

Inform those in your life who attempt to manipulate you with guilt that you are perfectly capable of handling their disappointment in you. For example, if Mama gets into one of her guilt acts with, *"You didn't do this,"* or *"I'll get the chairs, you just sit there."* Learn new responses like, *"Okay Mom, if you want to risk your back on a few chairs just because you can't wait a few minutes, I guess there is little that I can do to help you at this time."*

It will take some time, but the behavior of others will begin to change once they see that they cannot force you into choosing guilt. Once you defuse the guilt, their emotional control and their manipulation over you will be eliminated.

Guilt is a tool for manipulating others and a foolish misuse of energy. Worry, the other side of the coin, focuses exclusively upon the future and emanates from every terrible thought that you can possibly imagine, that may or that may not occur in the future. Worry also must be eliminated in order to live a more fruitful life.

WORRY

There is nothing to worry about, absolutely nothing. You can spend the rest of your life worrying about the future, but no amount of worry will change a thing. Worry is being helpless in the present as a result of situations that may or that may not occur in the future.

You must be careful not to confuse worrying with planning ahead. If you plan ahead and it contributes toward a more productive future, then that is a healthy situation. It is worry when you are in any way helpless in the present being overly concerned about events that have yet to occur.

Much of your worrying concerns situations that you have little control over. You can worry all you want about war, the economy, natural catastrophes, or illness [In fact, saturating your mind with constant worry is a major contributor to illness], but worrying will not bring about world peace, prosperity, or health. We have no control over any of these conditions by worrying. Affirmative action is the answer.

Moreover, the catastrophes we envision frequently turn out to be less frightening than they were in our imagination, and more often than not they will not occur at all. It was just our illusion.

Instead of worrying about potential problems, roll up your sleeves and get started this very moment, laying the ground work for a more productive future. Correct the things that you feel need to be corrected, and begin turning your dreams into reality.

Begin to view your present moments as your time to live and to enjoy, rather than fretting, fuming, or fussing about the future. When you catch yourself worrying, ask yourself, *"What am I avoiding now by using this moment to worry?"*

The best antidote for worry is action. Recognize the preposterousness of worry. Ask yourself over and over, *"Is there anything that will ever change for the better as a result of my worrying about anything?"*

*Worry never climbed a hill
or paid a bill
Worry never dried a tear
or calmed a fear
Worry never darned a heel
or cooked a meal
Worry never did a thing
but pain to bring*

Happiness is something we create in our mind,
something we search for, and so seldom find.

It is just waking up and beginning this very day,
smelling the roses, thinking what good we will say.

It is giving up thoughts that breed discontent,
accepting love, joy, and peace, as golden cement.

It is giving up wishing for things we have not,
completing our good thoughts, that mean a lot.

It is in knowing that life is radiant for us,
pursuing our tasks without fret, fume, or fuss.

Completing our destiny is ours to do,
finding contentment, and happiness too.

Designate thirty minutes in the morning and thirty minutes in the afternoon as your period of time to worry. Use these moments to fret about every potential disaster that you can squeeze into that time slot. Then, using your ability to control your own thoughts, postpone any further worrying until your next designated worry time. Allocate shorter and shorter periods of time for worrying. You will soon see the folly of using any time in this wasteful fashion, and you will eventually eliminate your worry time altogether.

Ask yourself this worry eradicating question, *"What is the worst thing that could happen to me, and what is the likelihood of it occurring?"* You will soon discover the absurdity of worry. Stop, turn to someone, and say, *"Watch me, I'm about to worry."* They will be so dumbfounded, since you will not be able to demonstrate the very thing that you do so well, so often . . . worry. The most effective weapon for wiping out worry is your own determination to take action and to banish this neurotic behavior from your life.

There are two days in the week that you must never feel guilty or worry about, two carefree days kept sacredly free from fear and from apprehension. One is yesterday, with its mistakes and cares, and with its aches and pains. Yesterday has passed forever beyond your control. The other day is tomorrow, with its possible adversities and blunders. Until the sun rises, you have no stake in tomorrow, for it is yet unborn. That leaves only one day, TODAY. Anyone can fight the battle for just one day. It is only when you add the burden of those two awful eternities, yesterday and tomorrow, that contentment will escape you.

Productively using your present moments is the key to eliminate guilt and worry from your life. Learn to utilize and to enjoy the present. Do not use up precious time and energy in helpless thoughts concerning the past or the future.

Look to the future,
look at the past,
worry and guilt,
guilt and worry,
what am I to do?

It won't occur
it doesn't last,
I'm going to wilt
wait and hurry,
what am I to do?

Believe in the future,
forget about the past,
get rid of your guilt,
stop your worrying
that's what to do!

This day belongs to all within the universe . . .
rich and poor, young and old, commoners and kings.
Time is not respectful of persons, places, or things.

Moment-by-moment, hour-by-hour
time keeps company with renegade and royalty
being bestowed upon us all with truth and equality.

Time is life's greatest asset,
yet not one hour may be stored away
nor can one beg, borrow, or buy one additional day.

Even the largest of fortunes cannot purchase
the fleeing moments, or change history;
once they are gone, they become only memory.

Time waits for no one.
It travels swiftly and silently in unison
with the rising and setting of the passing sun.

Like a vapor, it is here one moment, gone the next,
days disappearing, like the terminating dawn.
And we ask, "Where have all the moments gone?"

Today is ours with all the possibilities it offers,
twenty-four hours to use as we choose,
to spend at our discretion . . . to use or to abuse.

What will this day behold?
Will we be able to look back with satisfaction? Or,
have we lost forever golden opportunities left undone?

If challenges have been met with courage,
and warm relationships made along the way,
then we can say that we have lived, this very day.

Time is so very precious, we dare not waste a minute.
Cherish this day. Let not a pirate rob us,
for time is a treasure sanctimonious.

Chapter 16
Letting go of Fear

PROCRASTINATION IS FEARING THE UNKNOWN

Are you a procrastinator? Chances are, if you are like most people, your answer will be yes. However, the odds are that you would prefer not to live with all the anxiety that accompanies putting-things-off as a way of life.

Four neurotic phrases of the procrastinator that support putting-it-off behavior are: *"I hope things will work out," "I wish things were better," "Maybe it will turn out,"* and *"If I wait, it will improve."*

As long as you think in terms of delaying (hoping, wishing, maybe, or waiting) you will rationalize every situation that you wish to avoid. But it will not change any situation for the better.

Wishing and hoping are a waste of time, and no amount of either will ever accomplish a thing. They are merely escape clauses, preventing you from rolling up your sleeves and taking on the tasks that you have decided are important for you to fulfill. You can achieve anything that you set your mind to accomplish. A classic example of all too many relationships are couples avoiding their problems or justifying the avoidance of their problems by rationalizing . . . *"If we WAIT long enough and do nothing, MAYBE things will work themselves out. We'll just HOPE, WISH, and WAIT, and MAYBE things will work out for the best."*

To their dismay, nothing worked out for the better. The situation may have changed, but not for the better due to their lack of action.

The itching sensation that some people mistake for ambition is merely an inflammation of the wishbone. Itching for what you want doesn't do much good, you've got to scratch for it. Circumstances, situations, and events will only improve if something constructive is acted upon.

You are not always what you say you are. Actions are a better indicator of what you are than words.

The next time that you say that you will accomplish something, but know in your heart that you won't, keep those words in mind because they are an antidote for procrastination, and the antidote will improve your relationship with those around you.

Now that there is some insight into procrastination, you must begin to make some changes concerning the elimination of this self-destructive behavior.

If confronted with procrastination, make a decision to live five minutes at a time, instead of thinking of tasks in long range terms. Think about the present.

Start with a five-minute period of time, devoting all of your energy to doing that which you would like to accomplish, refusing to allow anything to inhibit its completion.

Stand up and get started on something that you have been postponing. You will find that most of your postponing was unnecessary, and that you may find the task pleasant once you give up your procrastination.

Simply beginning a task will help you to eliminate most of your anticipated anxiety. Ask yourself, *"What is the worst thing that will happen to me if I did what I am putting off right now?"* The answer may be so insignificant that you may instantly jump into action.

Look hard at your life. Are you doing what you would choose to do if you only had six months to live? If not, you had better begin to act now because, relatively speaking, that is all of the time that you have. Given the eternity of time, sixty years or six months makes little difference. Your total life span is but a mere speck in space. Delaying anything makes little sense. Be courageous. Set in motion all of the activities that you have been avoiding. An act of courage will eliminate all of your anticipated fears.

Yesterday, I looked
upon God's heaven
I wished that I may
I wished I might
I   wished   upon
a star last night
for things I liked.

Today, I am looking
for things I like
within my being
and creating them
within my mind
using the theorem
my value is within.

Avoid thinking that you must perform in a perfect manner or not do something at all. Doing something, even if it is not perfect, is far more important than doing nothing at all.

Decide not to be tired until the moment before it is time for you to retire at night. Do not draw upon fatigue or illness as an excuse to put off doing anything. One will find that by examining their reason for illness or exhaustion that their physical problems will magically disappear.

Eliminate the words **HOPE, WISH, MAYBE** and **WAIT** from your vocabulary. They are mental blocks that are preventing you from taking action. If these words creep in, substitute new phrases: Change, *"I hope things will work out,"* to *"I will do something to make things work,"* or *"I wish things were better,"* to *"I will do something to make things better,"* or *"Maybe it will work out,"* to *"I will do something to make it work out,"* or *"If I wait, it will improve,"* to *"I will start right now to fulfill my expectations,"* or *"When I get to feeling better, I will get started,"* to *"I will start right now, not allowing fatigue or illness to postpone any of my duties or desires."*

To change your world, do something constructive to change it, rather than complaining about it. Instead of wasting precious moments of life with all kinds of helpless anxiety from postponement, take charge of this negative behavior, and enjoy a more fruitful life.

BE A DOER, NOT A WISHER, A HOPER, OR A CRITIC

Oh, I wish I had a rainbow
I am waiting for a sign,
to brighten things around me
leaving shadows all behind.

Then I put aside the wishing
and the waiting time is gone.
I began making things happen
with some rainbows of my own.

JUST FOR TODAY

Just for today I will live through this day only, and not tackle my whole life's problems at once. I can do something for twelve hours that would appall me if I felt that I had to keep it up for a lifetime.

Just for today I will be happy. It assumes to be true what Abraham Lincoln said, that, "Most folks are as happy as they make up their minds to be."

Just for today I will adjust myself to what is, and not adjust everything to my own desires. I will take my luck as it comes and fit myself to it.

Just for today I will strengthen my mind, I will study, I will learn something useful. I will not be a mental loafer. I will read something that requires effort, thought, and concentration.

Just for today I will exercise my soul in three ways: I will do somebody a good turn and not get found out; I will do at least two things that I don't want to do just for the exercise; and, I will not show anyone that my feelings are hurt, they may be hurt, but for today I will not show it.

Just for today I will be agreeable. I will look as good as I can, dress becomingly, talk low, act courteously, criticize not one bit, not find fault with anything, and not improve or regulate anybody except myself.

Just for today I will have a program. I may not follow it exactly, but I will have one. I will save myself from two pests; hurry and indecision.

Just for today I will set aside a quiet half-hour all for myself, and relax. During this half-hour, I will develop a positive perspective of my life.

Just for today I will be unafraid. Especially I will not be afraid to enjoy that which is beautiful, and to believe that as I give unto the world, so the world will give unto me.

Chapter 17
Eliminating Anger

PREVENT IT

Is your fuse too short? You may accept anger as a part of your life, but do you recognize that it does not serve a useful purpose? Perhaps you have justified your short-fused behavior by saying something like, *"It's only human,"* or *"If I don't express it, I'll store it up and have an emotional crisis."* Anger is a frustrating part of your life, and needless to say, those around you find it equally frustrating as well.

Anger is an outpouring of pain caused by frustration, and is a choice as well as a habit. It is a learned reaction to frustration in which you behave in ways that you would prefer not to. In fact, severe anger is a form of insanity. You are briefly insane whenever you are not in control of your behavior.

You may be skeptical since you have heard that expressing your anger is healthier than keeping it bottled up inside of you. Yes, expressing your anger is indeed a healthier alternative to suppressing it, but there is an even healthier stance, not having the anger at all. In this case, you will not be confronted with the dilemma of whether to let anger out or to keep it in.

Like all emotions, anger is the result of your thoughts. It is not something that simply happens to you. When faced with situations that are not going the way that you want, you will tell yourself that circumstances should not be that way. So you will select a familiar angry response that you believe will satisfy that particular situation. As long as you think of anger as being a part of what it means to be human, you will have an excuse to accept anger, and you will avoid eliminating it.

Annoyances, irritations, disappointments, and rejections are all stimuli that you will continue to experience, since the world will never be exactly the way you want it.

But you do not need to respond to these situations with anger. Anger is a harmful emotional response to obstacles and must be eliminated in order to live a productive and joyous life.

The irony of anger is that it never changes situations for the better. It only intensifies another's desire to control you, and will make you look and feel foolish.

Anger, when used in any relationship, encourages others to continue to act as they have. Instead of choosing anger, you must begin to think of others as having the right to be different from the way that you would prefer. You may not like it, but you do not need to be angry about it. Your anger encourages others to react poorly, often causing physical stress and mental torture.

THE CHOICE NOT TO BE ANGRY IS YOURS?

Refusing to accept another's behavior or actions as having any influence over your emotions is the ultimate step in eliminating anger. You need to believe in yourself [refusing to allow others to control your life] so that you will stop hurting yourself with present moment anger. Anger must be eliminated. It requires new thinking and is accomplished one step at a time.

It is impossible for you to be angry and to laugh at the same time. Anger and laughter are mutually exclusive, and you have the power to choose either. Laughter is the sunshine of the soul, and without sunshine, nothing will live or grow.

When confronted with situations that provoke anger, become aware of what influences are working on your emotions. Then work on new thoughts, preventing an angry response, therefore creating a healthier you.

Get in touch with your thoughts at the time of your anger. Remind yourself that you are not required to think in terms of anger simply because you have done so in the past or because society has dictated it.

Postpone your anger for fifteen seconds, then explode in your typical fashion. Next time, postpone your anger for thirty seconds and keep lengthening the intervals. Once you begin to postpone or re-direct your anger, you will learn to control your anger, and you will eventually eliminate it altogether.

Remind yourself at the onset of your anger that everyone has the right to do and to say whatever he or she wants. Demanding that anyone be different will simply prolong your anger and intensify their retaliation.

It helps to be physically close to someone at the moment of your anger. One way to neutralize your hostility is to hold hands with someone, especially if it is the person who seemingly provoked your anger, despite your inclination not to do so. Keep holding hands until you have expressed or released your anger.

Defuse your anger for the first few seconds by identifying how you feel and how you believe those whom you are in conflict with feel. The first ten seconds are the most critical. Once you have passed this critical point, your anger will subside.

If possible, confront the person who you are in conflict with and explain to them your feelings and why you are angry. Ask them for their support and assistance in resolving this dilemma within you.

Keep in mind that most things will be met with some disapproval by someone. Once you accept disagreement as neither good nor bad, just different, you will not choose to be angry.

Remember: The expression of anger is an alternative to storing it up, but not having it at all is the healthiest choice of all. Once you stop viewing anger as natural behavior, you will develop a concern for eliminating your anger.

Children can be active, loud, and demanding. Getting angry will not make you or them feel any better, nor will it improve the situation. You have the advantage in helping children to make constructive choices.

Although, you will be hard pressed to alter their basic nature, your love and understanding will allow you to re-direct their choices by offering alternate positive solutions.

Instead of being an emotional slave to every frustrating circumstance, use the situation as a challenge to enhance it. This will reduce your time for anger and will help others to feel more comfortable. Anger inhibits effective thinking and will rob you of happiness.

Like all negative behavior, anger is allowing situations outside of yourself to control you. Forget what others say and do. Make your own choices [be your own hero], and do not let your choices be angry ones.

This day, all unexplored, belongs
to me to pattern as I choose.
The end result shall all be mine,
no matter if I win or lose.

The trifles that come crowding in
can neither vex nor irritate,
so long as I am aware
that I am the maker of my fate.

I find no satisfaction in pretense
behind a radiant sham.
The mirror in my heart gives me
a true reflection of who I am.

But this is a balm that I, far less
than just a tiny grain of sand,
can look within the universe for help
and know that love will lend a hand.

Chapter 18
Justice Trap

AN ILLUSION

Total justice appears not to exist. It never has and it never will. The world simply does not revolve that way. You only need to look at nature to view what appears to be injustice in the world. Floods, earthquakes, droughts, and tornados all seem to be unfair. People and the world around us seem to be unfair daily.

You have the choice to be happy or to be unhappy. But it has nothing to do with the lack of justice that you perceive around you.

When you find yourself saying, *"Would I do that to you?"* Change it to, *"Your views are different from mine, and you have the right to hold those views."*

The simple fact is that everyone is different and no amount of complaining will bring about any positive change. Only active and positive creativity will help.

When someone begins to criticize you, reply with this question, *"Do you think I need a critic right now?"* Or when you find yourself being a critic, ask yourself if you think he or she wants to hear your criticism and, if so, why? This will help to move you from being a critic to being a doer.

View productive living as being independent from what appears to be the injustices of the world. This will free you from the chains of feeling hurt when others behave differently from the way you prefer.

Revenge is another way of viewing injustice. Do not let what appears to be the injustice of others control your life. It is not the injustice that matters, it is the value that you place upon it that counts.

Be Positive!

Do you see doughnuts or just little holes?
Do you look for rainbows or ugly little moles?
Do you accent the positive or exaggerate the negative?
Are loving and kind or are you insensitive?
Do you try to understand or do you disagree?
Is your cup half-full or is it just half-empty?

Chapter 19
Exploring the Unknown

FIND ADVENTURE

Believe fully that all desires are within your reach. The entire gamut of human experience is at your fingertips, just for the choosing. These experiences are for you to enjoy, and these experiences will be multiplied many times over once you decide to venture into the unexplored or into the unfamiliar.

Opening up new horizons means surrendering the notion that it is safer to tolerate the familiar than to work on new adventures just because change is fraught with uncertainty. Avoid adopting the stance that you are fragile or that you are easily shattered by entering into areas that are new to you. This is a myth. You are a tower of strength and you will not break down or fall apart. Dare to venture beyond your comfort zone.

The fear of failing is often the fear of someone else's disapproval or ridicule. Let others have their opinions, which will have nothing to do with you. Be your own hero. Begin to evaluate yourself in terms of you, not in terms of others. Look for the abilities within yourself, not as better or worse, but simply different from others.

Become aware of avoiding the unknown. The fear of the unknown is just waiting to be replaced by new and exciting activities that will bring pleasure into your life. You do not need to know where you are going every instant as long as you are on your way.

BE ADVENTUROUS. Attempt something silly like going barefoot in the park or going skinny-dipping. Choose activities that you have been avoiding. Expand your personal horizon with new experiences previously avoided just because someone said that they were silly or, cannot or should not be done.

Give up the need for having a reason to do things. When people ask, *"What's your reason?"* your reply might be, *"just because I want to."*

Treat yourself to one of your fantasies, allowing yourself anything that you desire. Having enough funds for a two-week period is within reason for almost anyone [if you are willing to take the time and to work for it]. This way, you can make time for yourself to be as creative or adventuresome as you want without worrying about keeping your life intact. Most fantasies are achievable if you will eliminate your fear of the unknown and pursue your dreams.

Failure does not exist. Failure is simply someone's label for an action that they felt should have been done differently. Once you believe that no act must be performed in any specific manner, then failing becomes impossible. From making errors we will learn, yet we have learned to treasure success as the only acceptable standard.

Imagine failure as a description of an animal's behavior. It is impossible for an animal to fail because animals do what comes naturally; birds fly, fish swim, reptiles crawl. Natural behavior simply exists. So why not apply this same logic to human behavior and rid yourself of the fear of failure?

Doing your best is the cornerstone of the achievement neurosis. What is wrong with taking an ordinary bicycle ride or going for a common walk in the park? Why not have activities in your life that you like to do, without having to do your best.

This doing your best neurosis keeps you from engaging in new activities and from enjoying older ones. It is okay not to do things in a perfect manner.

We tend to shun all experiences that might bring about failure. Apprehension of failure is a big part of fearing the unknown. For example, anything that does not smack of guaranteed success is to be avoided. This is foolish thinking. Fearing failure means fearing both the unknown and the disapproval of others.

So why not fulfill your dreams, forgetting about guarantees, and what others expect of you? Do what is best for you.

Losing interest in life makes you potentially empty. Add a little spice of uncertainty. Make a selective effort to seek new ventures, even though tempted to stay with the familiar.

For example, order an untried meal at a restaurant. Why, because it would be different and you might enjoy it. Greet strangers with a smile and a simple, *"Good morning,"* or *"Good afternoon,"* on the streets, in a store or restaurant, at work, or anywhere for that matter, and watch their reaction. Some people will be confused while others will light up like a neon-sign, being silently thankful for your gift. You will be amazed at how good it will make you feel, when planting seeds of kindness with a smile.

A smile is a cheer to you and me,
the cost is nothing, it's given free.

It comforts the weary, gladdens the sad,
consoles those in trouble, good, or bad.

To rich or poor, beggar, or thief,
it's free to all, of any belief.

A natural gesture of young and old,
cheers on the faint, disarms the bold.

Unlike most blessings for which we pray,
it's one thing we keep, when we give it away.

To Strive
is to risk failure

To live
is to risk despair

To laugh
is to risk appearing the fool

To weep
is to risk appearing sentimental

To love
is to risk not being loved in return

To reach out
is to risk involvement

To expose feelings
is to risk exposing your true self.

THE GREATEST HAZARD IN LIFE IS
TO RISK NOTHING

Risks need to be taken in order to be fulfilled, to enjoy life, and to experience growth. Some suffering and some sorrow will be avoided by doing nothing, but you will not be able to learn, feel, change, and grow; which are all necessary for a meaningful and fulfilled life to exist. Only a person who takes risks will be free to enjoy life at its fullest.

Adventures do not require an explainable reason to be explored. They can be explored just because you want to. Looking for a justifiable reason deprives you of new and exciting adventures.

Thinking that you will accomplish anything for any reason, or for no reason at all, will open up new vistas of experiences and will help you to eliminate your fear of the unknown, adding enjoyment and happiness to your life.

Spontaneity means being able to attempt anything on the spur of the moment, just because it is different or because you might enjoy it. You may discover that you did not particularly enjoy that specific event, but attempting it was rewarding or exciting.

Being routine is being stagnant, and being aware of routine is the first step in changing it. The rigid never grow, and growth is life. The rigid tend to do the same old things throughout their life but the flexible keep engaging in new experiences.

Replace tradition with spontaneous thought and new ideas; discovering poetry, wit, faith, and knowledge. What a beautiful thought, toss tradition aside and the universe is yours to use as creatively as you choose.

Become the judge of your own conduct and learn to rely upon yourself to make your own decisions. Be your own hero. Cease leafing through a lifetime of policies and traditions for the answers. Sing your own song of happiness in any way that you choose, oblivious to the opinions of others.

Every day will be beautiful if you . . .

*Wake each morning believing in yourself
never losing faith in your dream.*

*Meet life with a song in your heart
smiling from your face supreme.*

*Find delight in life's simple pleasures
seeing rainbows, not the falling rain.*

*Get along with those around you, respecting
their creeds, yet staying true to your claim.*

*Give help and comfort in loving tone, being
a friend to those in need and all alone.*

*Make each day for you a new beginning
living the life that you will condone.*

*Find, that wherever you happen to be
will be a beautiful place for you alone.*

Chapter 20
Faith

THE ULTIMATE RESOURCE

There is a resource within you that offers unlimited power, a resource that probably is very much underemployed. If activated, this resource will give you the confidence and certainty to pull you through the toughest of times. It will get you to seize your life and to squeeze from it all of the wonder, joy, and fulfillment that you truly deserve. It is often the only resource left when you are at the *"end of your rope."* And it lies within you right now, at this very moment. What is this resource? It is the one unique thing that the human spirit can utilize at any given moment . . . **FAITH.**

Faith is a requirement for all human progress. Without faith you will not be able to accomplish anything. We prepare ourselves to the best of our ability, but finally we must trust that somehow we will do fine, without this willingness to trust and to act we will not even have the courage to leave our home.

In relationships, many people fail to commit out of fear. *"What if this person is not the right one?"* *"What if someone better comes along?"* These fears will kill a relationship before it begins. To have anything of value, at some point you must decide to trust your value system, and to believe that all things will work out for the best. You must believe that you will do whatever is necessary to find value in the decisions that you make.

Humans have a natural conflict, a conflict between faith and fear. If fear wins, your dreams will surely die. If faith wins, your only limitations will be the scope of your imagination and commitment to daily discipline and flexible action.

Whatever level of success that is achieved in life will be due to an evolution of an ever-increasing level of faith; faith in yourself with absolute commitment to persist and to give your all; faith in people with their caring, understanding, and desire to grow.

Have faith in your GOD (or, however you identify your supreme power or entity), and have faith in finding your purpose in life; have faith in the ability of the human mind and spirit to expand.

Faith will give you the power to overcome the difficulties and the tragedies in your life. It will give you the willingness to trust even though you may not understand why things happen [it is all for the best] and to look actively for the advantage in any given situation that appears to be confronting you. Without faith, little of what you value most in life would not exist.

FAITH IS THE ABILITY TO TAKE THE INVISIBLE AND MAKE IT VISIBLE

Everything that you see around you was at one time merely an idea (something invisible) and that someone had enough faith and courage to persist until it became a visible reality. They turned their vision into a physical reality through absolute faith, action, flexibility, and working with others.

Focus on where you want to go, not on where you have been or on what you fear. Remember that what you get in life is what you focus on.

Hope and faith are not the same. Hoping and doing nothing, produces nothing. You need active faith. Active faith is deciding what you want, committing to it, and then resolving that [no matter what] you will find a way to make it real. This requires active, consistent, flexible action. Even when you experience temporary disappointments, you must be willing to believe that in the long run all of your deepest needs and desires will be met.

POWER OF PRAYER by D.R. Hunt
Honorary Doctorate of Theology, USA

Prayer is the spiritual communication between one's self and one's higher-power. To be effective one must muster enough faith and belief to produce, through thought and prayer, certain desired results, e.g. forgiveness, comfort, health, inner-peace, relationships, financial stability, correcting problems and situations, and most important desiring the well-being of others.

The most identifiable biblical prayer world-wide is the LORD'S PRAYER. Jesus spoke to the multitudes in his *'sermon on the mount'* giving them a pattern of how to pray. This was heard by and recorded by Luke, one of Jesus's twelve disciples. Luke recorded it in Aramaic in the biblical book of Luke 11:2-4. Below the author D.R. Hunt re-translated this prayer from his understanding, experiences, and research, including examination of original manuscripts.

LORD'S PRAYER (as defined by D.R. Hunt)
Introduction - We honor & pray to you O'Lord.

Our Spiritual and Loving Heavenly Father, Creator of the Heavens and the Universe; who gave us life and freedom of choice. We honor you and we present to you our pleas.

The Seven Petitions - *We honor you O'Lord & We express our prayers and pleas to you.*

1-We honor your Holy name.
2-Your Heavenly Kingdom will come to earth like it appears and is honored in Heaven;
3-For all to observe and to accept your Devine Desire which is to receive your Eternal gift of life.
4-Give us Wisdom each day to follow your guidelines; to love, serve and obey your instructions.
5-Forgive us O'Lord of our wrong doings and help us to forgive all those who have wronged us.
6-Help us to avoid all evil persuasions, and
7-Protect us from all wicked forces that continually plague us.

Doxology - *A hymn of praise to you O'Lord for you are the Kingdom, the Power & the Glory.*

What is the Kingdom?

According to Luke 17:21: For behold, the Kingdom of God is in your midst.
You are the Creator of all things; creating man from the earth and breathing life into him.
You are the supreme example of life, one of which, you created Adam in your own likeness.

What is the Power?

You are the force that creates and binds all things, and You are the power that controls all things.
You are the Ever-Loving-Heart that can forgive all, and the power to answer all pleas.
You gave your son authority to judge man, and to write into the *Lamb's Book* all entering Heaven.

What is Glory?

You are the source of Heavenly Saints and Angeles; who proclaim praises of Love, Comfort and Blessings to all that believe in your Spiritual Force; forever and ever; so be it, and make it so.

Amend

NAMASTE-God bless the divinity in you.

They told him that it couldn't be done,
with a smile, he went right to it.
He tackled that which couldn't be done,
and found out that he could do it.

What you can do or dream you can, begin it,
only engage, and the mind will go undefeated.
Courage has genius, power, and magic in it,
just begin it, and the work will be completed.

Too often, we judge too soon the results of our faith [delays are not denials]. If we have long term faith, all will serve us. Also remember that sometimes we do not receive that which we have perceived. We may receive something much greater than expected. Have faith in your mind and spirit.

If you fill your hours with regrets over misperceived failures of yesterday, and with unfounded worries over the problems of tomorrow, you will not have enough time left in today to be thankful for what you have.

So, how can you have faith and not ignore your challenges? By using the three steps of active faith: View things as they really are; envision these things as you want them to be; then, create what you envision, making it a reality.

*In pursuing your dreams
there will be moments
when it seems as if
your dreams are lost.*

*It is at that moment that you must have
faith in the person that you truly are,
believing that you have within you, the
ability to overcome, whatever the cost.*

*When your dreams materialize,
you will then realize what a
creative and productive person
you have uniquely embossed.*

GOD GRANT ME THE SERENITY TO

ACCEPT THE THINGS

THAT I CANNOT CHANGE

COURAGE TO CHANGE

THE THINGS THAT I CAN

AND THE WISDOM

TO KNOW THE DIFFERENCE

Serenity Prayer

Chapter 21
Decision Making

NO GUARANTEES

The question of right or wrong, as it applies to decision making, has nothing to do with theological beliefs, moral issues, or philosophical principles.

Discussions inevitably become contests that result in one person being right and the other being wrong. You have heard comments like, *"You always think you're right,"* or *"You never admit being wrong."* People are different and view things from different perspectives. If one must be right, then a breakdown in communication is the only predictable outcome. If you need to end a debate, you might say, *"I don't understand your point of view at this time, but you have the right to hold your opinions."*

Taking away rightness or wrongness makes decision making less frustrating. For example, if you select Decision-A then these are the more likely results, while Decision-B will probably bring about this outcome. Neither is wrong. One is simply different from the other. Just choose the one that you believe will best suit your needs.

It's very important to remember that there are always at least two choices to every potential decision that you need to consider. And, after making your decisions, you still have more choices or alternatives to consider.

You will reduce your indecisiveness by viewing potential outcomes as being neither right nor wrong, good nor bad, but simply different. Unfortunately, there are no guarantees, regardless of the correctness of your decisions. Just do the best you can.

One very important decision that you make daily is whether to be happy or unhappy. It is your choice and not the result of another's behavior or actions. What others do must not concern you. Instead, what should concern you is the amount of value that you place [or not placing any value] upon others and their actions.

Instead of thinking, *"They shouldn't do that,"* consider this question, *"I wonder why I bother myself with what others do?"* Blaming is a device that is used to avoid taking responsibility.

Blaming is a fraudulent use of time. When someone attempts to place blame or guilt upon you, politely ask them, *"Would you like to know if I need to hear what you are telling me right now?"*

The tendency to focus on others will go to the opposite extreme when it surfaces as hero-worshiping. In this case, you look to others to determine your own worth (if so and so does it, then I should do it). Hero-worshiping is a form of self-repudiation. It places more importance upon others than upon yourself.

While there is nothing self-defeating about appreciating others and their accomplishments, it becomes negative behavior when modeling your behavior from another's point of view. You may be acting foolishly if you look outside of yourself for an explanation of how you should feel or act.

BE YOUR OWN HERO

When you are free from blaming and free from hero-worshiping, you will move forward from the external world to the internal you, and you will become free to make your own decisions.

Making decisions to blame, to hero-worship, or to be unhappy are all in the category of negative attitudes, wasting time and energy, and robbing you of a happy and fulfilled life. Start now, directing your focus upon positive thoughts, and begin to enjoy life with all its love and splendor.

One of the main inhibitors of decision-making is pain. We have all experienced it. Most people link pain to attempting changes in their lives because they unconsciously believe that these changes will only be temporary, or that the end result will not turn out as desired.

RAISE YOUR STANDARDS. Make a decision concerning what you will no longer settle for. Write down all the things that you will no longer tolerate, as well as what you are absolutely committed to becoming, achieving and creating. Now link massive pain to not meeting those standards, and tremendous pleasure in living by your commitments.

CHANGE YOUR LIMITING BELIEFS. Changing your relationships, your job, your health, etc., begins with the simple step of changing your belief that change is possible and that the end result will be as desired.

If you raise your standards but you do not really believe that you will meet them, then you have already sabotaged yourself.

Your beliefs are like unquestioned commands telling you what you will and what you will not do. They shape every action, thought and feeling that you experience.

Changing your beliefs is paramount to making real and lasting changes in your life. Without changing your beliefs for the better, you can raise your standards as high as you like, but you will never have the conviction to back them up. Empowering your beliefs, this sense of certainty, is the force behind all great success.

CHANGE YOUR STRATEGY. In order to keep your commitment, you need the best strategy for achieving results. When you set a higher standard and believe that you will absolutely achieve it, you will figure out the strategies to make it happen.

One of the simplest ways to discover how to produce a result more quickly is to find a role model, someone who is already getting the results that you desire, and tap into their knowledge and resources [I do not mean becoming that person], be your own hero.

If you are going to make change last, there is a philosophy beyond these three basic principles that you must adopt. It will shape every aspect of your life. It is one that will determine the quality of your relationship with your family, your friends, and be responsible for your economic success, physical vitality, and energy. It is a fundamental discipline to live by daily that will give you an incredible sense of joy, peace and contribution.

Every truly successful person lives by this philosophy, which is: The only way you will truly experience long term change and personal success is if you

CONSISTENTLY INCREASE THE QUALITY OF YOUR LIFE

This will only be accomplished by a commitment to

CONSTANT AND NEVER ENDING IMPROVEMENT

Most people strive to reach a certain level of quality [a certain income or position] and then they think that they can relax. What a myth. They become stagnant and wither away.

Goals are designed to make you grow, expand and improve. As soon as you achieve one goal, immediately set a new one or you will lose momentum and your joy.

You and I can only feel truly happy when we are growing. And, we only feel growing when we are constantly improving and expanding our awareness.

The key here is to make

GRADUAL, CONSISTENT IMPROVEMENT ON AN INCREMENTAL LEVEL

in every aspect of your life. If you really want to change your life long term, you cannot just maintain what you have. If you are not improving you will fall short. The problem is, most people wait until they have a major problem [they're vastly overweight or their relationships are in shambles] then they attempt to change things overnight. For a week, they will do everything that they can think of to improve their situation, but gradually they fall back into their same old habits.

Remember: Long term success is created only through small, gradual, daily enhancements and refinements of each area of your life. This has unlimited power to create the quality of life that you have always dreamed of. The great news is that it is believable and that it is achievable.

Write down all of the different ways in which you will implement this philosophy; in your job, in your relationships, in your own personal growth, etc. What will you do today to raise your standards, to change your beliefs, and to learn new strategies and skills, for producing the results that you desire? Remember: The quality of your life is in direct proportion to the quality of your commitment to constant and never-ending improvement in every aspect of your life. Enjoy your growth and remember to live it with passion.

In life, there will be many paths to follow, many decisions to make. Never be afraid to make decisions. Your decisions may not always turn out in the way that you had planned. But, if they were the best decisions based upon your understanding at the moment, then that is the most that anyone has the right to expect of you. Never regret the past, it is over and beyond your reach. Do not waste it, learn from it.

Believe in yourself and never lose sight of your dreams. You have the ability to accomplish anything that you set your mind to. Focus on what you want and muster enough faith that your decisions will carry you through.

The secret is: **ENVISION** what you want; concentrate enough **FAITH** in yourself that you will make the precise decisions to create what you envision; then, take **ACTION** to create that which you had envisioned, turning it into a reality.

If you can go through life loving yourself, you will have succeeded in making the greatest decision of all.

It's not always easy to know
which path to follow, which
decision to make, or what to do.

Life is a series of new horizons,
new dreams, new days, and new
opportunities that come into view.

Remember these things:
Dream it, create it, and
discover how special are you.

Be positive, for your focus will affect
the outcome of all things that you do, and
give yourself credit where credit is due.

Make some new progress every day.
Begin, believe, and become;
making way for your dreams to come true.

Don't short change your qualities
or any of the things that are
so great and unique unto you.

Invest the time it takes to reach out
for your dreams: Life is too short . . .
here one moment, then away she flew.

Don't be afraid: No mountain is
too tall, no valley is too deep,
nothing is too difficult for you to do.

Ask for help when you truly need it: Seek
answers, which the universe holds within,
then thank the creator for your revenue.

Chapter 22
Declaring Your Independence

BE FREE

Leaving the psychological nest is one of life's more difficult chores. The dependency viper interferes with life in many ways. Psychological independence means freedom from obligatory relationships. It means freedom from doing something that you would not choose to do if the relationship did not exist.

Leaving the nest is especially difficult because society teaches us to fulfill certain expectations in special relationships that include parents, children, authority figures, and loved ones.

Leaving the nest means becoming your own person, living and choosing the situations that you want. It does not mean breaking off in any sense of the word. If you enjoy your way of interacting with someone, and it does not interfere with your beliefs or goals, then it is something that you should cherish rather than abandon.

Psychological dependence, on the other hand, means that you are in a relationship that involves limited choices; a relationship that you feel obliged to be in or, are forced to do things that you cannot condone.

Furthermore, you will resent being poorly treated and you will resent being forced to conduct yourself contrary to your beliefs.

Wanting some kind of relationship is not unhealthy. But if you need a relationship, or you are forced into it and subsequently feel resentment, then you are on the road to self-destruction.

It is the obligation that is the problem, not the relationship itself. Obligation breeds guilt and dependency, while choice fosters love and independence. There is limited choice in a psychologically dependent relationship, consequently there will always be indignation and ill feelings in any such alliance.

Being psychologically independent involves not needing others [I did not say wanting others, I said needing others]. The moment that you need others, you become vulnerable, a slave. If the one that you need leaves, or changes their mind, or dies, you are then forced into helplessness, collapse, or even death.

Eliminating dependency starts with your family, with the way your parents dealt with you as a child, and the way you deal with your children. How many psychologically dependent thoughts do you carry in your head today? How many of them do you force onto your children or others around you? What do you want for your children? Would you prefer them to have self-esteem, to have self-confidence, to be free of negative behavior, to be fulfilled, to be happy? Of course you would.

You will only inspire such an outcome by being that type of person yourself. Children learn from the behavior of their role models. If you are full of guilt and you are unfulfilled in your life, instructing your children not to be is telling them a hypocritical story. If you display low self-esteem, you will teach your children to adopt the same attitudes for themselves. Even more significant, if you make your children more important than yourself, you are not helping them. You are merely teaching them to put others ahead of themselves and to take a back seat, while remaining unfulfilled.

You cannot force your children to have self-confidence. They acquire it by observing you as an example, and by you giving them the tools or skills of understanding, creativity, and responsibility.

By treating yourself as the most important person, and not always sacrificing yourself for others, you will assist others to believe in themselves, creating their own self-confidence.

From the very beginning, children want to do things for themselves. For example, *"I can do it myself,"* or *"Watch me, mommy, I can do it without any help."* On and on the signals come. And while there is a great deal of dependency found during those early years, there is also a distinctive drive toward autonomy from almost the first day.

Leaving the nest, in a psychologically sound environment, involves neither crisis nor turmoil; it is a natural result of productive living. When guilt and fear of disappointment colors the nest, these qualities may continue throughout your life; sometimes to the point that your marriage relationship becomes one of parenting of each other, rather than two individuals sharing an equal footing.

In families that focus on independence, movement towards being one's own person is seen as normal, rather than as a challenge to anyone's authority. The result is family members who want to be together, rather than feeling obligated to be together. There is also a respect for privacy, rather than a demand to share everything. Hence, the parent can go off alone occasionally and not feel obliged to always be there for their children.

In healthy families, the woman enjoys a life of her own beyond motherhood. She will model effective living for her children, rather than living her life for or through them. The parent must feel that happiness is paramount because without happiness, there will not be family harmony.

You may have resolved your dependency on your parents, perhaps you recognize your children's need for independence and are encouraging it, however, if you are one of those persons who left one dependent relationship with your parents and entered another dependent relationship when you became married, then you have a negative area that needs guidance.

Marriage is that relationship between a man and a woman in which independence is equal, the dependence is mutual, and the obligation is reciprocal. There they are, the two ugly words, dependence and obligation, which accounts for the state of marriage and rate of divorce in our country.

A relationship based upon love allows each partner to be what he or she chooses without expectations or demands. It is a simple association made up of two people who love each other so much that neither would expect the other to be something that they would not choose for themselves. It is a union based upon independence. Imagine a union with the one that you love in which each can be whatever he or she desires.

Keep in mind that it is not your responsibility to make others happy. Others are responsible for their own happiness. You are responsible for your own emotions and feelings, and so is everyone else responsible for theirs. You alone have the responsibility of controlling your feelings. This does not diminish your responsibility to be thoughtful and courteous to others.

You may experience fear when breaking away from dependent relationships. If you ask those upon whom you are emotionally dependent, you will discover that they will most admire those who think and who act for themselves. You get the most respect for being independent from those who try the hardest in keeping you subordinate.

The nest is a beautiful place for a child to develop. In turn, leaving the nest will be even more beautiful, as viewed by the one leaving as well as by the one watching the take-off, if it is accomplished with love and with understanding.

Chapter 23

Magnify Your Energy

TRUST, FOCUS, ACT

Your energy level is proportional to the energy that you deposit into your belief system. You will have as much energy as you put your mind to.

If you believe, focus, and commit [take action] to a higher degree of energy, that is what you will create.

It is interesting to note that there is an intimate relationship between your emotional well-being and your physical health, and that the state of each is in direct correlation to your general well-being and your level of energy.

BELIEVE THAT MAGNIFYING YOUR ENERGY IS POSSIBLE. You must unite enough faith for you to believe that a high-energy level is conceivable and is achievable.

FOCUS ON THE LEVEL OF ENERGY THAT YOU DESIRE [the sky's the limit]. Eradicate all obstacles from your Mind, Body, and Soul that you perceive to be curtailing your energy.

COMMIT TO ACHIEVING HIGH ENERGY. Make a list of the internal and external forces that you perceive to be affecting your energy. Empower yourself to banish all barriers from your list that are inhibiting your well-being and your energy.

Listed below are some of the potential problem areas for your consideration. These may seem very basic, but are many times overlooked.

NUTRITION. Proper nutrition is required for the maintenance and growth of every cell and organ within your body. You don't have to go to extremes or go on special diets, just eat balanced non-fatty meals and drink plenty of fluids [not alcohol]. And, if you feel it is necessary, reinforce your diet with supplemental vitamins, minerals, or other nutrients that you feel are lacking in your body. If you feel the need to have snacks between meals, try eating fruits or vegetables.

REST. Peaceful rest is essential for the rejuvenation of your Mind and Body. How you feel upon awaking in the morning is a good indicator as to the quality and quantity of sleep that you require. [Quality is much more beneficial than quantity]. If you awake vibrant, alert, and full of energy, then you will have been successful.

The quality of your slumber is equated with the condition of your Mind and Body just prior to your sleep. If you are at peace within yourself, then your sleep will be peaceful, and you will awake with peace.

If your body is in pain or your mind is full of undesired garbage [guilt/worry/fears], then you will awake un-rejuvenated and lacking energy.

You need to let go of your problems [fears], and to grant freedom to those that you need to set free, before retiring each night.

EXERCISE. Exercise is essential for maintaining your body in a healthy and vibrant state. Also, your Mind needs to be exercised to promote growth, which is necessary to sustain your life in a meaningful way.

Your exercise program should at least consist of:

Fast walking to increase your heart rate and to assist your digestive system; performing stretching exercises to tone and stretch your muscles giving them vitality and elasticity; flexing your joints to maintain their mobility; and, rehearse breathing exercises, taking in life-sustaining oxygen to cleanse your cells, to enhance the efficiency of your lungs, and to clear your Mind.

Exercise your Mind by learning something new and useful. Read something that requires effort, thought, and concentration. Solve problems by making decisions, and expand your awareness and knowledge by reading, watching and listening. Be open to new understandings. This will contribute towards your growth and well-being.

STRESS. Maintaining a safe level of stress is mandatory for a joyous and tranquil way of life. Anytime that you experience excessive stress your well-being is being inhibited, preventing you from making quality decisions and being fully functional.

ENVIRONMENT. Sometimes it is necessary for you to remove yourself from situations or people to find a peaceful place to meditate in order to rejuvenate your life; by defining your purpose; by directing your focus; by calming your soul; and, by resting your mind and body.

Satisfy your mind, body and soul by transporting your being to a place of tranquility; such as, mountains, deserts, the sea, libraries, art galleries, botanical gardens, parks, concerts, restaurants, sunsets, sunrises, watching the clouds go by, whatever works best for you to align your true-self with the natural wonders and abundance of the universe; to promote balance, peace and tranquility within yourself, becoming one with the universe.

MEDICAL MALFORMITIES. Genetic and birth defects, mental disorders, injuries, infections, diseases, aging, nerve and organ malfunctions must all be studied by professionals to identify if any of these disorders are inhibiting your well-being and to have them corrected if they are.

If your exercise program contains one or more of the following, stop it immediately for it's hazardous to your health: Bending over backwards. Dodging responsibility. Flying off the handle. Juggling facts. Jumping to conclusions. Pulling hair.

Remember that if your eyes, teeth, or feet hurt, your whole body will be in pain that will prevent you from making wise decisions and living a meaningful life. Have annual medical check-ups of your eyes and teeth and if your eyes, teeth, feet, or any other body function bothers you seek medical advice as soon as possible.

co co luo

WHAT IS MEDITATION?

Meditation is an enrichment to your soul. Its meditative state is the natural outcome of yoga and tai chi, and the spiritual benefit of meditation is supreme bliss and enlightenment. Progress towards meditation and meditative techniques have several benefits at the physical and mental levels; cleansing the mind of negativity, therefore, purifying the body.

When your mind focuses on a particular part of the body, the blood flow to that part increases and cells receive more oxygen and other nutrients in abundance, improving body luster and general health.

Studies have found a direct correlation between concentration exercises (meditation, prayer, yoga, tai chi) and performance levels. Meditation strengthens the mind; it comes under control and is able to provide effective guidance to the physical body to effectively execute all of its functions. Psychological Exercises are a powerful way of improving concentration, mental stability, and improving physical health.

Though meditation is usually recognized as a spiritual practice, it also has many physical and mental health benefits. Yoga, tai chi, and praying techniques are being implemented in the management of life threatening diseases; in reversal of mental illnesses; in accelerated learning programs; in perceptions and communications beyond the physical in solving problems; and in the management of lifestyle problems.

Some benefits of meditation are lower oxygen consumption, decreased respiratory rate, increased blood flow, slower heart rate, increased exercise tolerance, deeper level of relaxation, regulating high blood pressure, reducing anxiety, decreasing muscle tension and headaches, building self-confidence, increasing serotonin production that influences mood and behavior (low levels of serotonin are associated with depression, obesity, insomnia, headaches, etc.), placates chronic diseases like allergies, arthritis etc., reduces Pre-menstrual Syndrome, helps in post-operative healing, and enhances the immune system. Research has revealed that meditation increases activity of *'natural-killer cells'*, that kills bad bacteria and cancer cells.

There are two types of meditation; active and passive. Active meditation relates to activities of everyday life such as walking, working, eating, etc. This in-fact is the aim of Yoga, to experience a meditative state in everyday life that has the effect of increasing multiple performance levels as work is done with more efficiency and energy.

To achieve Active Meditation, passive meditation is required that involves taking time out to be placed in a quiet, peaceful setting to perform Meditation techniques. This is called passive as it involves withdrawing ourselves in a calm, sitting postures to achieve a meditative state that can help us in our active life. The aim of passive meditation techniques is to still the mind from wavering and distracting (negative) thoughts and gradually transport one's consciousness into the consciousness of the universe, where all is one.

Choose a time when you are not likely to be disturbed. Settle in a place that has fresh air. You may sit in any of the meditative poses depending on your comfort level, and to stay in that pose for a desired duration of time. Begin by focusing on something non-threatening. This will relax you and help break your stress response. Concentrate on a subject that appeals to you; it could be a flower, a word, or the flame of a candle. Notice how your thoughts wander. Don't attempt to control them. Observe them with detachment. Within a few weeks, you will notice a marked difference in your capacity to focus. This is the stepping-stone to awareness. You are now becoming aware of your ability to control your mind; to cleanse your mind of negativity and to increase your ability to focus. This will greatly enhance your mind and body functions, giving you joy and good health.

Lift your head
see all around you
see who you really are.

Be amazed at
the glow of your being
that outshines every star.

Feel the inspiration of
every mountain, sea, and shore
being inspired as never before.

On a clear day
you can see forever
and forever and evermore.

co co luo

WHAT IS YOGA?
By Co Co Luo Certified Yoga Trainer & Financial Advisor
www.cocosyoga.com

Yoga is a group of physical, mental, and spiritual practices or disciplines that originated in ancient India. Yoga, in general, is a spiritual practice or discipline that helps the individual unify the mind, body and heart. The Hatha yoga is one of six major schools of yoga that is commonly taught in America.

Yoga practice emphasizes proper diet, processes to internally purify the body, proper breathing, body alignment, and exercise routines consisting of bodily postures and meditation.

The aim of Hatha yoga has traditionally been the same as those of other varieties of yoga. They include special physical powers or bodily benefits, such as, slowing age effects, meditation (mind cleansing giving inner peace), and spiritual liberation.

In the 20th century, techniques of Hatha yoga, particularly physical postures, became popular throughout the world as a form of physical exercise for relaxation, body flexibility, strength and personal concentration. Yoga's combined focus on mindfulness, breathing, and physical movements brings many health benefits.

Yoga participants report better sleep, increased energy levels, muscle tone, relief from muscle pain and stiffness, improved circulation and organ function, mind clarity relieving stress and increasing inner peace, enhancing brain function, and overall better general health. The breathing aspect of yoga can benefit heart rate and blood pressure as well.

Yoga is a direct experience of the vastness of all life and of all things. You will feel at peace at the end of a yoga class because there is a natural realignment of your body that leads to a natural realignment of your perception of life and of who you are.

Genuine yoga will change your life, your habits, your body, your health, your mind, your breathing patterns, your attitudes, and your outlook on life. You will develop wisdom of how your body works most efficiently. You will learn how your conscious and unconscious mind can either support or harm you, and then later, your deeper wisdom naturally gets revealed. The benefits of Yoga will come to those who practice it with passion and regularity.

WHAT IS TAI CHI?
by Chinese Tai Chi trainer Simon Shen
& Transamerica Financial Advisor
simon.shen@tfaconnect.com

Tai Chi Chuan, translates as *"the supreme ultimate force,"* is a martial art discipline often called a *"moving meditation"* since the movements are slow and deliberate, and is taught more as a meditative and health enhancing practice than as a martial art discipline.

Tai Chi is the Taoist belief in a universal energy called chi. Chi is believed to be the binding life force in the universe moving through invisible channels throughout the body called meridians. In Chinese medicine, proper energy flow promotes good health and obstructed energy flow causes poor health.

Certain breathing techniques, meditations, and body movements are thought to cultivate and enhance the chi (energy life force).

While Tai Chi may offer senior practitioners inner peace, scientists also value Tai Chi for its fundamental physical benefits. In addition to improving balance, flexibility, and mental agility, Tai Chi also reduces falls, the largest preventable cause of injury and death among senior adults. One way to help the aging have a long and vital life, according to researchers, is to help protect seniors from injuries or worse.

Tai Chi is one of the most exciting interventions because it benefits balance, mobility and memory. It aids the muscular system, coordination, equilibrium, and brain function.

Because Tai Chi requires attention, memory, and learning components to master its physical movements, its benefits go far beyond improving mobility and reducing falls. It increases mental mindfulness and promotes social interaction because Tai Chi is usually practiced in a group setting.

In this low-impact, slow-motion exercise, you go without pausing through a series of motions named for animal actions. As you move, you breathe deeply and naturally, focusing your attention as in various forms of meditation. Tai chi differs from other types of exercise in several respects. The movements are usually circular and never forced, the muscles are relaxed rather than tensed, and the joints are not fully extended or bent. Tai chi can be easily adapted for anyone, from the most fit to people confined to wheelchairs or recovering from surgery.

WHAT IS QIGONG?

Qigong (pronounced *Chee-gun*) means energy cultivation. It is a discipline that combines meditative and physically active elements and is the basic exercise system within Chinese Medicine. Qigong exercises are designed to help preserve your **Jing** (*kidney spirit*), strengthen and balance the flow of **Qi** (*life-force energy*), and enlighten your **Shen** (*human psyche*). Its dynamic movements, breathing techniques and meditations have **Yin** and **Yang** aspects: The Yin is being it; the Yang is doing it. **Yin Qigong** exercises are expressed through relaxed stretching, visualization, and breathing, while, **Yang Qigong** exercises are expressed in a more aerobic or dynamic way. They are particularly effective in supporting the body's immune system.

Qigong's physical and spiritual routines move Qi (*energy*) through the body's twelve primary channels called Meridians plus eight extra channels; balancing, smoothing and strengthening the flow of life-force energy.

Chinese medicine uses Qigong exercises to maintain health, prevent illness, and extend longevity, for Qigong is a powerful tool for maintaining and restoring harmony to the body's organ systems, essential body substances, and life-force energy meridians. Qigong is also used for non-medical purposes, such as for fighting (*martial arts*) and for pursuing inner-peace enlightenment; pursuing harmony with the Universe.

Anyone of any age or physical condition can do Qigong: From the very fit to those with disabilities can pursue healthfulness and enjoy its benefits.

We each have inherited imbalances that we cannot control but with which we must work at. That is why for some people it is easier to achieve balance and strength than it is for others. But whatever your nature, Qigong can help you become the most balanced person you can be, filled with vitality & joy.

The Qigong routines are very gentle but the results can be very powerful. Many people over age sixty in China practice Qigong and Tai Chi to promote flexibility, strength, balance and inner-peace, prompting harmony with the Universe.

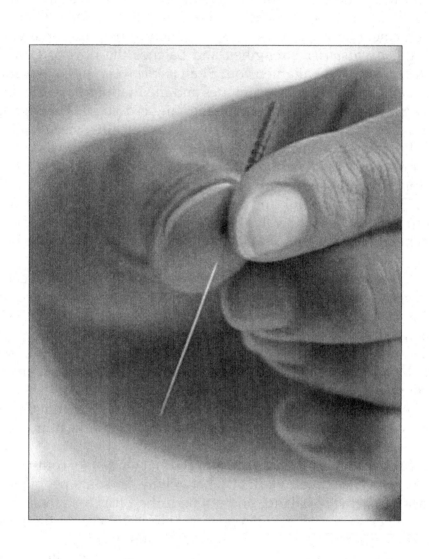

WHAT IS ACUPUNCTURE?

Acupuncture is a complete Chinese medical protocol focused on correcting imbalances of chi (energy) along body meridians that control the health of all cells and organs. It incorporates inserting fine needles into the skin to stimulate the flow of energy throughout the body. From its inception in China more than 2,500 years ago, acupuncture has been used traditionally to prevent, diagnose and treat disease, as well as to improve general health.

The traditional explanation for acupuncture's effectiveness is that it increases or unblocks the flow of energy (known as qi or chi) throughout the body. Acupuncture's traditional role of balancing energy addresses a wide range of disorders, and the understated mechanisms that may be responsible for its overall benefits to health.

Because the goal of acupuncture is to promote and restore the balance of energy, that flows throughout the body, the benefits of acupuncture can extend to a wide variety of conditions, from emotional disorders (anxiety and depression) to digestive complaints (nausea, vomiting, irritable bowel syndrome). It can be beneficial for pain syndromes due to an injury or associated with chronic degenerative diseases such as rheumatoid arthritis. It can also be helpful in treating neurological problems like migraine headaches or Parkinson's disease, or as a rehabilitation strategy for individuals who suffered a stroke. Respiratory conditions, including sinusitis and asthma have been relieved with acupuncture, as have many gynecologic disorders and infertility. Acupuncture has also proved beneficial for reducing fatigue and addictions, and for promoting overall well-being.

Studies in the U.S. indicate that acupuncture can help relieve chronic low back pain, dental pain, migraine headaches, fibromyalgia and symptoms of osteoarthritis. It has been shown to assist in the treatment of emotional pain syndromes such as post-traumatic stress disorders, as well as, controlling chemotherapy-induced nausea and vomiting.

Typically, the first acupuncture visit involves a comprehensive health history assessment. Questions that are included may seem strange, but in Traditional Chinese Medicine (TCM) that encompasses acupuncture, herbal medicine, massage and other forms of health improvements.

Energy flow and whole-body interaction are the keys to diagnosing all physical disease. For example, the practitioner may ask to examine your tongue, eyes and your breath, feel your pulse to help determine energy flow, or ask many questions related to bowel habits and diet, even if these seem to have nothing to do with the primary complaint.

Acupuncture is often performed within the context of TCM, which typically offers dietary interventions, bodywork, and the taking of herbs in combination with acupuncture treatments.

Acupuncture is frequently used in conjunction with *"cupping"* and *"moxibustion"* that are Asian techniques designed to increase energy (blood flow) to a particular area of concern.

Acupuncture can be used effectively with other therapies including various forms of massage, chiropractic or osteopathic manipulation, as well as, different movement therapies such as tai chi, yoga and qigong.

WHAT ARE CHAKRA CENTERS?

The Sanskrit word Chakra literally translates to wheel. In yoga and meditation, this term refers to wheels of energy throughout the body. There are seven main Chakra Centers, which align the spine, starting from the base of the spine, continuing up the spine, to the crown located on top of the head.

To visualize a Chakra Center in the body, imagine a swirling wheel of energy where matter and consciousness meet, and functions as a vortex of spinning energy interacting with various physiological and neurological systems in the body. Chakras are energy centers within the human body that help to regulate all processes, from organ functions to the immune systems to emotions. This invisible energy, called Prana, is the vital life force that keeps us vibrant, healthy, and alive.

These swirling wheels of energy correspond to massive nerve centers in the body. Each of the seven main Chakra Centers contains bundles of nerves and major organs, as well as, our psychological, emotional, and spiritual states of being. Since everything is moving, it is essential that our seven main Chakra Centers stay open, aligned, and fluid: If there is a blockage, energy cannot flow. Think of something as simple as your bathtub drain. If you allow too much hair to go into the drain, the bathtub will back up with water, stagnate and eventually bacteria and mold will grow, so is it with our bodies and the chakras.

Keeping a chakra open is a bit more of a challenge, but not so difficult when you have awareness. Since mind, body, soul, and spirit are intimately connected, awareness of an imbalance in one area will help bring the other areas into balance. Each chakra has its own vibrational frequency, that is depicted through a specific chakra color, and governs specific functions that helps in making you well, making you human.

Awareness to which of your chakras are out of balance is key to aligning them. Our bodies are in constant flux between balance and imbalance. Unless you have an apparent problem in one area of the body, imbalances can be difficult to detect. That being said, it's good to bring awareness to your body/mind and start to learn its signals and clues. For example, frequent constipation can indicate a blockage in the first chakra. A recurring sore throat leaves clues to a blocked fifth chakra. Frequent headaches around the area of the forehead may mean your sixth chakra is blocked. The foundation to a healthy system consists in opening and balancing the chakras in order to create a sustainable, harmonious flow of energy.

You must learn that with every thought there is a reaction. This response can either energize or decrease your life force. Negative thoughts are against the Godly plan of loving, therefore, bad life conditions can be attracted.

Increasing your chakra energy

Simply take a shower with sea salt to clear and cleansed your energy systems. Rub the sea salt into your skin while setting your intention to cleanse your aura, washing away anything that does not belong to you. By using your intention, your consciousness directs the energy where it needs to go.

Close your eyes and take a few deep breaths and simply imagine standing under a magical waterfall, which can wash away any negative energies and impurities. See and feel the warm water falling down onto your head, shoulders and running over your body until all negativity is washed away, leaving you energized and cleansed, alive and vibrant, joyous and loving.

Visualize and imagine your energetic boundaries stretching outward a few inches around your body. Once you can feel or sense it, visualize the energy around your body as a dense protective color like purple. You want to train yourself in such a way that you can quickly and easily visualize the color around you so that you can quickly protect your energy field when you need it the most.

The root chakra, which is located at the base of your spine and that connects you into the Earth, gives you a feeling of safety and protection when it's energetically strong. The quickest and easiest way to strengthen it is to simply take off your shoes and walk barefoot on the Earth. If you don't have the opportunity to walk barefoot in nature, the next best thing is to take your shoes off (you can do this anywhere), stand erect and visualize a grounding cord from the soles of your feet right into the Earth's core. Do this for a few minutes until you feel more grounded and more at home within your body. Being grounded in your body is a natural protection against other people's energetic influence.

The first three chakras, starting at the base of the spine, pertain to matter and are physical in nature.

Root Chakra 1 is located at the base of the spine and is Red.
Functions: Safety, grounding, and right to live. This chakra is our stability, security, and our basic needs. It encompasses the first three vertebrae, the bladder, and the colon. When this chakra is open, we feel safe and fearless.

Sacral Chakra 2 is located above the pubic bone and slightly below the navel and is Orange.
Functions: Emotions, creativity, and sexuality. This chakra is our creativity and sexual center, and is responsible for our creative expression.

Solar Plexus Chakra 3 is located slightly above the naval and is Yellow.
Functions: Will, social-self, and power. This chakra means

lustrous gem and it's the area from the navel to the breastbone. The third chakra is our source of personal power.

Heart Chakra 4 is located at the center of chest and is Green/Pink. Functions: Compassion, love, and is the connection between Matter and Spirit. It unites the lower chakras of matter and the upper chakras of spirit. The fourth chakra is spiritual and serves as a bridge between our body, mind, emotions, and spirit. The heart chakra is our source of love and connection. When we work through our physical chakras, or the first three, we can open the spiritual chakras more fully.

Throat Chakra 5 is located on the throat and is Light Blue. Function: Personal truth and expression. This is our source of verbal expression and the ability to speak our highest truth. The fifth chakra includes neck, thyroid, parathyroid glands, jaw, mouth, and tongue.

Third Eye Chakra 6 is located in mid-forehead between the eyebrows and is Indigo. Functions: Extrasensory perception, intuition, and inspiration. It is referred to as the *"third eye"* chakra and is our center of intuition. We all have a sense of intuition but we may not listen to it or heed its warnings. Focusing on opening this chakra will help you hone this ability.

Crown Chakra 7 is located at the top of the head and is Violet. Functions: Wisdom, divine existence, and universality. The Crown Chakra or the *"thousand petal lotus"* chakra is located at the top of the head. This is the chakra of enlightenment and spiritual connection to our higher-selves, others, and ultimately to the divine.

Chapter 24
Portrait of a Positive Person

The individual who is void of negative behavior may seem to be a fictitious character. However, being free from self-destructive behavior is not a mythological concept, rather it exists as a real possibility for all of us. Being fully-functional is within the grasp of each and every one of us.

Individuals free of negative behavior are different from the run of the mill individuals, primarily because of their positive attitude towards life. While they look very much like everyone else, they possess very distinct qualities. They do not fit neatly into any particular job description, geographic location, educational level, financial status, or ethnic background.

These individuals love virtually everything about life. They are comfortable doing almost anything and do not waste time complaining or wishing things in their life were otherwise.

They are enthusiastic about life, wanting to acquire all they can from it. There is an absence of grumbling, moaning, and even passive sighing. Ask them what they do not like and they would be hard-pressed to come up with an answer. Certainly they can admit to making mistakes, but they do not waste time tormenting themselves over past events. They go on with their life, changing adversity into challenge.

Freedom from fear (worry, guilt, and procrastination) is a hallmark of these healthy individuals. They will not become angry. However, they will adapt to a situation, rather than becoming upset.

They are not always calm. However, they are unwilling to spend present moments agonizing about things they cannot change, they have the courage to change the things they can, and they have the wisdom to know the difference.

They are not threatened by the unknown. They seek out experiences that are new and exciting. They savor the present, being aware that the present is the only period of time that they have control over.

They do not postpone anything, they are doers. These individuals enjoy life simply because they see the folly of waiting to enjoy it.

These healthy individuals are noticeably independent. They have left the nest. While they feel strong love and devotion toward their family and other relationships, they see independence as superior to dependence in all relationships. Their relationships are built upon mutual respect for the right of individuals to make their own decisions.

They place a high premium on privacy. It is difficult for dependent or unhealthy people to hang onto them because they are adamant about their freedom. They want others to be independent enough to stand on their own, being able to make their own decisions, and to live their own lives, although, they will lend their support if it is needed.

These individuals function without approval or applause from others and are unusually free from the opinions of others, almost uncaring what others do.

They do not need to be loved by everyone, nor do they need to be applauded or to have approval to authenticate their worthiness in order to insure their happiness.

They recognize that they will always meet with some disapproval, which only means that others have different points of view.

They are not rebels but will make their own choices, even if those choices conflict with others.

They do not engage in small talk simply because it is the polite thing to do, or because they cannot find anything else to do, or because they feel lonely.

They know how to laugh, and know how to create laughter. They find humor in virtually all situations, and they can laugh at themselves as well. They are not hostile in their humor, refraining from the ridicule of others to create laughter. They do not laugh at people, they laugh with them. They do not know how to be offended by anything that is human. They love themselves, therefore they accept themselves for who they are.

They love nature. They especially love mountains, deserts, the sea, sunsets, rainbows, waterfalls, and virtually all flora and fauna. They love the beauty and naturalness of the universe.

They have insight into the behavior of others. What may seem complex and indecipherable to others is seen clearly by these healthy individuals. Their lack of emotional involvement with problems allows them to surmount barriers that remain insurmountable to others. They have insight into themselves as well, and they can recognize immediately when others attempt to use or abuse them.

These are not sickly people. They do not believe in being rendered helpless by colds or by headaches. They never go around telling others how badly they feel, how tired they are, or what diseases are currently inflicting their bodies. They are healthy individuals who treat their bodies well.

They respect themselves, and consequently, they eat well, rest when needed, and they exercise regularly. They refuse to embrace the infirmities that render most individuals helpless.

Another hallmark of these fully-functional individuals is their honesty. They are neither evasive with their responses nor do they pretend or lie about anything, including the sin of omission. They do not cloud their messages in carefully worded phrases designed to please or to deceive.

While they are private people, they will avoid distorting the truth to protect others. They behave in ways that are sometimes perceived as selfish, while in fact, they are simply allowing others to stand on their own.

They do not talk about people, they talk with them. They do not blame others. They help others and themselves by placing responsibility where it belongs.

They are neither gossips nor spreaders of erroneous information, and they only speak good of others.

These individuals have exceptionally high levels of energy because they are excited about living. They can muster tremendous surges of energy for completing tasks that they choose to be involved in.

They aspire to the old saying that, *"if you can't say anything nice, don't say anything at all."*

They do not know how to be bored, instead, they are aggressively curious. They search for knowledge, and they want to learn each and every moment of their lives.

They exercise their mind regularly by solving problems, by making decisions, and by expanding their consciousness, striving for unity with the universe.

They are not afraid to take risks. They are willing to attempt things that are different or exciting, thereby increasing their awareness.

They do not argue or enter into hot-headed debates. They simply listen to others, state their views, and recognize the futility of convincing others to be or to act differently. They will simply say, *"That's all right, we're just different, we don't have to agree."* Then let it go at that, without feeling the need to win or to lose arguments, or to discover the rightness or the wrongness of an event. They view all people equally and they do not place others above themselves.

They do not demand justice at every turn. When they observe individuals with more privileges, they view that situation as beneficial for those persons.

When playing opponents, they want them to perform well rather than wishing a poor performance in order to win by default. They want to be victorious by their own merit.

They are motivated by the desire to grow, and treat themselves with respect. They have no room for self-pity, self-rejection, or self-hate.

They may not have problem-free days, but they are free from emotional immobility as a result of their problems. They live each moment of every day to its fullest. They stand tall, with their heads high, and their eyes wide open [taking in all of the goodness within the universe].

By using your own present moments in maximum fulfillment, you too, can be a fun loving individual, being free from the chains of fear. What a delightful concept ... freedom from fear and being free to love.

YOU CAN MAKE THAT CHOICE NOW

Keep ascending the mountain of cheerfulness and to each day scatter the seeds of kindness along your way the best you can, and should a mist appear hiding the mountain top, continue courageously until you reach the sun-tipped heights of your destiny.

There is nothing that I can give to you that you do not have already, but there is much that, while I cannot give to you, you can take: No Joy can come to you unless your heart can find peace in today, **TAKE JOY**; No Peace lies in the future, which is hidden in this present moment, **TAKE PEACE**; gloom of the world is but a mere shadow, behind it, yet within reach is Love, **TAKE LOVE.**

Laugh a little, sing a little
as you go your way.
Work a little, play a little
Do this every day.
Give a little, take a little
never mind a frown.
Make your smile a welcomed thing
all around the town.
Laugh a little, love a little
Skies are always blue.
Every cloud has a silver lining
and it is all up to you.

Laugh and the world will laugh with you. Love and the universe is yours. This is just the beginning, for

TODAY IS THE FIRST DAY OF THE
REST OF YOUR LIFE

Take time, or time will take you
and drain your strength away.

Take a minute or maybe two
throughout your busy day,
for slowing down to meditate
from worldly things to pray.

Take time to think about
the greatest things of all,
taking time to work things out
before the last curtain call.

Take time to slowly stroll
gathering from the universe,
to nourish a hungry soul
finding love in golden verse.

Take time to roam the grass
enjoying the flowers and trees,
wandering and pondering at last
on wonders such as these.

Slacken your pace
to see the view,
and take your time
*   or*
TIME WILL TAKE YOU!

BOOKS OF RELATED INTEREST

Three Magic Words by U.S. Andersen

When Helping You is Hurting Me by Carmen Renee Berry

Living, Loving & Learning by Leo F. Buscaglia

Loving Each Other by Leo F. Buscaglia

The Incredible Credible Cosmic Consciousness Diet by Harvey Cohen, Ph.D.

How to Survive the Loss of a Love by Melba Colgrove

Anatomy of An Illness by Norman Cousins

The Healing Heart by Norman Cousins

Your Erroneous Zones by Dr. Wayne Dyer

Pulling Your Own Strings by Dr. Wayne Dyer

The Sky's the Limit by Dr. Wayne Dyer

Good-Bye To Guilt by Gerald G. Jarnpolsky

Love is Letting Go of Fear by Gerald G. Jampolsky

Teaching Only Love by Gerald G. Jarnpolsky

When Bad Things Happen to Good People by Harold S. Kushner

Male & Female Realities by Joe Tanenbaum

I Love You, Let's Work It Out by David Viscott, M.D.

For your financial freedom visit
http://infinitesuccessalliance.com

Do you want to write your own book or make your current book
a bestseller?
Bestsellerguru.com

Yoga for body, mind, and spirit
cocosyoga@gmail.com
www.cocosyoga.com

Life coaching by coachjimmyg.com